TUGS
TODAY

As part of our ongoing market research, we are always pleased to receive comments about our books, suggestions for new titles, or requests for catalogues. Please write to: The Editorial Director, Patrick Stephens Limited, Sparkford, Near Yeovil, Somerset, BA22 7JJ.

TUGS TODAY

MODERN VESSELS AND TOWING TECHNIQUES

Foreword by Captain C. E. J. Dowswell, Chairman, British Tugowners Association

M. J. Gaston

PSL

Patrick Stephens Limited

First published in 1996

British Library Cataloguing in
Publication Data
A catalogue record for this book is available
from the British Library.

ISBN 1 85260 521 9
Library of Congress Catalog Card Number: 96-75820

Patrick Stephens Limited is an imprint of
Haynes Publishing, Sparkford, Nr Yeovil, Somerset, BA22 7JJ.

Typeset by
Character Graphics (Taunton) Ltd.

Printed and bound in Great Britain by
Butler & Tanner Ltd, Frome and London

Contents

Foreword

by Captain C. E. J. Dowswell, Chairman, British Tugowners Association.

Tug enthusiasts, both professional and amateur, will welcome this sequel to Mr Gaston's *Tugs and Towing* published in 1991. In the intervening five years much has happened in the shipping world to bring the towage industry into the public eye. The publication of the "Donaldson" report after the *Braer* incident and the wide publicity following the *Exxon Valdez* affair have heightened the public awareness of the importance of tugs. Understandably the public's knowledge of tugs is limited. Books such as these will do much to inform and enlighten.

Jack Gaston's experience and knowledge of the towing industry combine with his skill as an author to present a factual and unbiased account of towage as it is today. His books are recognised as authoritative in an industry that has lacked documentation, and as such will be welcomed by all those interested in the complexities of our specialised marine field.

Acknowledgements

I would like to thank most sincerely my many friends and acquaintances in the towing industry for their great encouragement, support and above all patience. Without their assistance in answering my many questions and the ready access they have given me to their tugs, this work could not have been completed. Special thanks are due to the staff and crews of Howard Smith Towage & Salvage, Cory Towage Ltd, Red Funnel Tugs, Smit International, Johannes Ostensjo AS, Bureau Wysmuller, Shetland Towage Ltd, International Transport Contractors, McTay Marine, Damen Shipyards and many others.

My grateful thanks are also due to Captain David Brown who has been a great source of encouragement and expertise throughout. His scrutiny of the final draft manuscript in such detail was particularly valuable. I am also indebted to the many companies and private individuals who have so readily supplied photographs and other material – all of which are acknowledged individually beneath the relevant illustrations. Tim Rolfe has given invaluable help in preparing the line drawings, showing great patience in trying to interpret my sometimes vague instructions.

Finally, my grateful thanks are due once again to my wife Ann and my family for tolerating the many long absences and periods of silence while the final manuscript was being completed.

M. J. G.

Introduction

Tugs Today aims to describe in some detail the modern towage industry and its vessels, worldwide. During the past decade economic pressures have forced considerable changes on this specialised and interesting branch of shipping. Tugs continue to have many roles in shipping, the offshore oil industry, marine civil engineering and other related industries. In order to meet the ever-changing commercial demands made upon it the industry has turned increasingly to sophisticated modern propulsion systems, new technology, advanced electronics and innovative operating methods.

One of the most important services provided by tug companies is to give assistance to ships entering and leaving port. There are, and probably always will be, ships that can only be handled safely in port with the aid of tugs, and similarly there are harbours that are only accessible to ships of any size when tugs are on hand to assist them. In this scenario the use of a tug represents an unwelcome added cost to the ship owner. Consequently, there is continuing pressure to operate tugs more cost effectively with smaller crews and reduced running expenses. In ports frequented by very large ships, or those carrying hazardous cargoes, there are also increasing demands for tugs with more power and greater agility. Most modern tug fleets are much smaller than their predecessors, but in general they employ vessels that are considerably more sophisticated with relatively small crews.

Recent accidents involving very large oil tankers, where massive pollution of the coastal marine environment occurred, have led to the introduction of escort tugs and emergency response vessels in many locations throughout the world. In the majority of cases it has fallen to the tug operator to provide specially designed and equipped vessels to undertake this relatively new task. The escort tug and its operation has therefore become an important preoccupation for the towage industry, and continues to be the subject of heated discussion on the legal and practical issues involved.

Salvage and the towage of ships and large floating objects over long distances has always been one of the more emotive aspects of the towage industry, and often seen by the public at large as exciting and perhaps a little glamorous. It is a harsh fact that in commercial terms this part of the industry has changed beyond all recognition, with the dedicated salvage tug rapidly becoming a very rare species indeed. Its modern replacement is called upon to be extremely versatile, and the role of the long-distance tug is increasingly taken up by the powerful oil rig supply vessel. The latter is well established in the offshore oil industry, which demands sophisticated vessels capable of working increasingly in remote and hazardous areas, where oil exploration would have been unthinkable even a decade ago.

In spite of the changes and developments in the industry as a whole there are many aspects of towage that are changing at a slower rate and in which more traditional vessels and methods remain predominant, and these are not ignored in the present book. Less sophisticated vessels are still widely employed in many parts of the industry. Tugs of various shapes and sizes are also in use towing barges on the waterways of the world, assisting fishing vessels in small harbours, working with dredgers and floating plant on marine civil engineering projects, and carrying out a whole range of similar tasks. The small, efficient, tug/workboat has become a powerful force in many of these roles and has played an important part in the evolution of series-built vessels of all sizes.

It is the foregoing towage scene that *Tugs Today* attempts to describe, in a manner suitable for those with a passing interest in the subject, yet sufficiently stimulating for those engaged in the industry. It is intended as a natural successor to my previous book, *Tugs and Towing*, published in 1991, which had just that aim and was well accepted. A very similar format has been adopted and the technical information, although similar, has been completely revised. As the following pages will illustrate, a great deal has happened in the towage industry since 1991. This book is not an instruction manual – it is a broad view of a very specialised sector of the shipping industry and its vessels, allowing comparisons to be made, in a way that will hopefully prove interesting. Chapter 1 describes the basic types of vessel currently in use and gives some insight into their design and construction. The chapters that follow deal with propulsion systems and the array of specialist equipment found aboard the modern tug, and describe in more detail how the various types of tug are employed. Many oil rig supply vessels have a very real towing capability and are included in this overview. Although the content of *Tugs Today* has a natural bias towards European vessels and their operation, considerable effort has gone into ensuring that examples are drawn from the industry world wide.

With a subject such as the towage industry, which has become so dependent on technology, it is easy to overlook the human element. The successful operation of tugs, whatever the type or role, continues to depend heavily on the highly skilled tug master and crew. As yet no amount of sophisticated equipment can replace the judgement and experience of the people responsible for operating these vessels, often in difficult weather and tidal conditions, at any time of year, day or night. In many of the photographs, taken in pleasant summer conditions, tugs are shown working sedately in near perfect conditions. That work often has to continue, during high winds and rough seas, in mid-winter or Arctic conditions, in the middle of the night, alongside a ship of possibly a quarter of a million tons. It is still people that skilfully handle the tug or go out on deck and handle freezing ropes to make a towing connection.

Glossary of terms

Amidships – A term referring to the centre portion of a vessel. Also used to describe the position of a vessel's rudder to indicate the "straight ahead position".

Anchor-handling – The process of laying and retrieving the anchors for oil rigs and similar pieces of offshore floating plant.

Azimuthing – A term frequently used when describing a propulsion unit where a conventional propeller is used, but is capable of being "steered" or rotated (usually through a full 360 degrees) about a vertical axis to direct thrust at any angle in relation to the hull.

Bitts – Posts or similar fittings of heavy construction used to secure ropes for mooring or towing. Often mounted in pairs. See also Bollard.

Bollard – A single post or similar fitting used to secure ropes for mooring or towing. See also Bitts.

Bollard pull – The tractive effort produced by a tug or other towing vessel when pulling against a static object (a bollard). May be expressed in tons (Imperial) or tonnes (metric).

Bow thruster – A means of providing directional thrust at the bow of a vessel to improve its handling characteristics whilst manoeuvring.

Brake horsepower (bhp) – The actual power generated by a diesel engine under test conditions, when coupled to a dynamometer (brake).

Bridle – Two short lengths of wire rope or chain cable, assembled to form a "Y" and used to make the connection between a vessel being towed and the tug's towline. The term is also used in some areas to describe a Gog rope.

Bulwark – The side plating of a vessel above deck level.

Capstan – A revolving drum used to assist in the hauling of ropes and towlines.

Chaser – An appliance used in anchor-handling to locate a buried anchor and provide a means of securing a pennant to heave it from the seabed.

Combi-tug – A conventional screw tug with a steerable thruster unit located at the bow.

Dead ship – The term used by tugmen to describe a ship that is without her own means of propulsion and steering.

Deadweight – The weight in tonnes of cargo, stores, fuel, passengers and crew carried by a ship when loaded to its maximum loadline.

Dry towing – A method of transporting vessels that are unwieldy and difficult to tow by loading them on a specially designed barge.

Fairlead – A fitting attached to the deck or bulwarks of a vessel to act as a guide for ropes, to prevent chafing and other damage.

Fender – A pad of resilient material used to protect the tug's hull against damage from contact with other vessels and structures. Commonly manufactured from rubber, wood, rope or vehicle tyres.

Flanking rudders – Additional rudders located forward of the propeller(s).

Flying bridge – An open control position located above an enclosed wheelhouse.

Girding – A term used to describe a tug being capsized by the action of a ship or other vessel she is towing. Capsizing may occur when the towline is abeam of the tug (at 90 degrees to her centreline) and sufficient force is generated by the action of the tow to pull her over bodily. Also described as Girting.

Gob rope – See Gog rope.

Gog rope – A rope used in ship-handling work with European-style, conventional screw tugs to control the position of the main towline as a precaution against girding (capsizing). Also known as Gob rope, stop rope or bridle.

Gross tonnage – A volumetric measurement of the interior of the hull and other enclosed spaces. 100 cubic feet is equal to 1 gross ton. The formula used to measure a vessel can vary with the registration authority.

Ground tackle – An anchor and its associated tackle, used in salvage work to provide additional pulling power when refloating a vessel aground.

Handy – A term used to describe a vessel that is manoeuvrable and responds readily to her controls.

Heaving line – A light line or rope with a weighted end designed to be thrown by hand. Used when making a towing connection to haul across a messenger or towline.

Indicated horsepower (ihp) – The calculated, theoretical power output of a steam or diesel engine.

Messenger – A small-diameter rope used to haul a towline or rope of a larger size.

Molgoggers – See Norman pins.

Norman pins – Pins or rollers that can be erected at the tug's after bulwarks to guide the towline and prevent it from passing over the vessel's beam. Also known as Molgoggers or stop pins.

Nozzle (propulsion) – A device mounted around the propeller to augment thrust.

Pendant – A short length of steel wire or man-made fibre rope attached to the end of a towline to resist wear and chafing. The word pennant is used in some regions to describe the same item.

Pennant – The steel wire rope used to lay and recover anchors. See also Pendant.

Pitch (propeller) – The theoretical distance the propeller will advance during one complete rotation.

Push knees – Structures fitted to the hull of a tug or multi-purpose vessel to enable it to push barges with a minimum risk of damage to either craft.

Rubbing band – A band of resilient material fitted around the hull of a vessel as protection against impact damage.

Ship-handling – Giving assistance to ships in confined waterways when they have insufficient manoeuvrability to proceed safely unaided.

Skeg – A fixed rudder-like fin fitted beneath the after hull of a tug to provide additional directional stability. Also used on towed barges to improve their handling characteristics.

Splice – A method of joining two ropes or forming a permanent loop. Carried out by separating the strands of the rope and forming a connection by interweaving the free ends.

Spring – A section of rope forming part of a towline designed to introduce an element of elasticity, thus reducing the shock loads involved in towing. The term also describes a mooring rope intended to prevent fore and aft movement of a vessel.

Stop pins – See Norman pins.

Stop rope – See Gog rope.

Stopper – A device used to secure temporarily a towline while changes or repairs are carried out.

Superstructure – The wheelhouse, bridge accommodation and similar structures built above deck level.

Tackle – A combination of pulley blocks and ropes or lines used to provide a mechanical advantage when hauling or lifting.

Tow beams – Protective bars or tubular structures erected over the tug's after deck to prevent the towline fouling fittings or deck equipment. Sometimes passing over the entire deck from bulwark to bulwark.

Towline – A rope used in towing to connect the tug to its tow. May be of steel wire rope or man-made fibre rope.

Tractor tug – A tug with its propellers or propulsion units located beneath the hull, forward of amidships, to pull rather than push the vessel along.

Wheelhouse – The main control position from which the tug master commands the vessel.

Winch – A mechanical device used to haul, control and store ropes during towing or lifting.

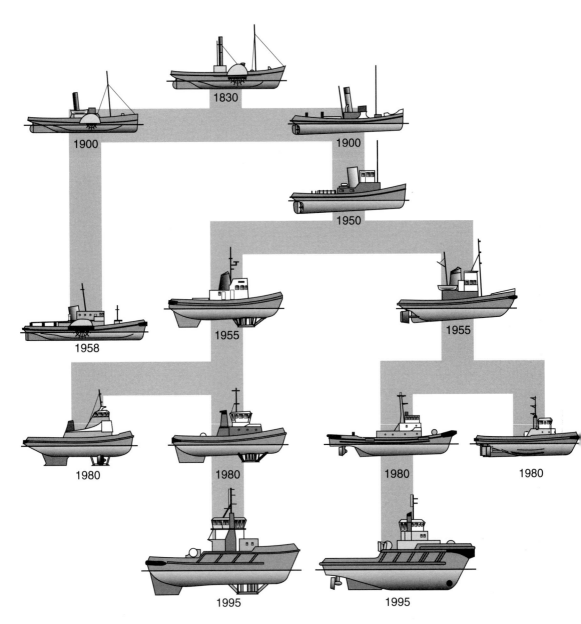

The chart plots in very broad terms the evolution of the ship-handling tug and its propulsion systems in Europe, starting with the first commercial paddle vessel in 1830. By the 1900s screw and paddle designs were well established in a form that was to remain virtually unchanged until WW II. Development of the paddle effectively ceased with the introduction of eight diesel-electric tugs in Britain in 1958. By the 1950s diesel power was becoming common and by the middle of the next decade Voith Schneider propulsion and Kort nozzles were appearing in some numbers. By the 1980s Azimuthing tractors, Voith tractors, conventional screw and a small number of stern drive vessels of Japanese origin were in use in Europe. Development of escort tugs in the mid 1990s resulted in direct competition between Voith Schneider and stern drive designs.

CHAPTER 1

Tug design and construction

The purpose of this chapter is to describe as simply as possible the different basic tug types, and to show how the use of various modern propulsion systems has influenced hull configuration and, to some extent, superstructure design. Some attention is also paid to the construction of modern tugs, and the features in their design that make them unique among small ships. The propulsion systems, their controls and engines are often utilised in different ways and in more than one type of tug, so they are described separately and in some detail in Chapter 2.

From its inception in the 1830s the tug developed rapidly for some 60 years. Paddle-driven vessels were soon superseded in many areas by those equipped with screw propellers, and by the turn of the century an established basic configuration had emerged. The vessels had steam-powered machinery, but many of the principles of hull and superstructure design remain valid to this day in conventional screw-driven vessels. In the years that followed, construction methods changed, propulsion machinery was refined and eventually the diesel engine was universally adopted by the industry at large. In spite of much experimentation with engines, propellers and nozzles to enhance thrust, the first radical departure in tug design did not come until 1954. In that year the first ship-handling tug fitted with a Voith Schneider cycloidal propeller was put into commercial use, bringing a whole new concept to the industry. In subsequent years tug development continued to accelerate dramatically, with a number of alternative propulsion systems soon to become available. Each has its merits and some can be utilised in a variety of ways. At the present time the tug owner is faced with a bewildering array of options when choosing a new vessel.

There are many established rules that govern the hull design of all ships and boats. Some of those rules have been in use since the days of the early steamship and determine, for example, a direct relationship between a vessel's length, beam and speed. The underwater shape, size and volume of a hull each play an important part in the vessel's performance and handling characteristics. These principles apply to virtually any vessel that moves through the water, and for the first century or so tug construction deviated very little from those basic rules. The introduction of novel propulsion systems, employing other than conventional screw propellers located beneath the vessel's stern, has complicated matters considerably. Additional space may be required to accommodate bulky propulsion units, or the underwater shape of the hull may

The steam tug Francis Batey *of 1914 represents the type of vessel which readily comes to mind to many people when tugs are mentioned. This basic 'traditional' design remained virtually unchanged, in steam and motor tugs, until the 1950s, in Britain and Europe. This particular vessel was operated on the River Tyne by Lawson Batey Tugs Ltd and was not scrapped until 1968.*

have to be modified to improve water flow to the propellers or to enhance a particular feature of the tug's performance. In steam-driven vessels, where comparatively little power was available, tug masters made good use of the weight and underwater shape of their vessels when controlling a tow. Modern tugs, with much lighter machinery, have less actual weight but frequently incorporate features built into the hull design to achieve improved performance by using similar dynamic effects. The paragraphs that follow describe the various types of tug and explain how designs have changed to accommodate the propulsion systems currently installed and to suit their intended use.

Basic tug types
Conventional screw tugs
The term "conventional screw tug", in the context of this book, means a vessel propelled by one or more screw propellers fitted to rigid propeller shafts located at the stern. This type of propulsion is generally regarded as the norm in ships and was standard in virtually all tugs prior to the 1950s. A great many tugs are still built using this form of propulsion, but new types of propeller, the use of thrust-enhancing nozzles and sophisticated rudder systems have greatly increased in recent years. Although the vast majority of older tugs still in service around the world are driven by conventional screw propellers, there are now very few new vessels that employ a single, open screw propeller without some form of nozzle or steering device fitted. An exception is the single screw "Combi"-type of tug, which is mentioned later in this section.

Sun Essex *is typical of many single screw ship-handling tugs that continue to give good service in Britain. Owned by Howard Smith Towage & Salvage and currently in use at Southampton she is a vessel of 272 gross tons, 2072 bhp and 35 tons bollard pull built in 1977.* (Author)

Grace McAllister *is a traditional American style ship-handling tug built in 1968 and still in service with* McAllister *Brothers Inc of New York. She is a vessel of 292 gross tons powered by a General Motors main engine of 3160 bhp.* (Michael Vincent)

Twin-screw designs are now much more common and are used widely in ship-handling, anchor-handling and deep-sea tugs, offshore supply vessels and small tug/workboats. In most modern applications propulsion nozzles of either the fixed or steerable type are used, often with innovative rudder systems. Open propellers are rare in new European twin-screw vessels, but are still preferred by some operators in the United States of America and elsewhere. In terms of design, the hull form of a modern conventional screw tug has changed little from

The fleet of Smit Harbour Towage of Rotterdam includes a number of modern twin screw tugs of the same type as Smit Polen, *a 2400 bhp vessel built in 1986. The 236 gross ton vessel is propelled by twin controllable pitch propellers rotating within fixed Kort nozzles.* (Author)

The hull form of Raslanuf VII *is typical of many modern vessels, with few compound curves and relatively straight forward construction. This example is a twin screw tug 27 metres in length and 2350 bhp.* (Author)

its predecessors. Length, breadth and hull configuration are chosen to suit the vessel's application. In some ports the size of ship-handling tugs may be restricted by the dimensions of locks or other limiting features of a confined dock system.

During the early post-war period diesel-powered tugs were built using a hull design known as "Hydroconic". The hull was of a double-chine configuration, built mainly from simple welded plates with little need for complex compound curves. Hulls of this type proved cheap to produce and had good performance characteristics while towing and running free. Modern designs often follow similar principles, adapted to accommodate recent advances in propulsion technology. In all cases the underwater shape is designed to provide unrestricted water flow around the rudders and propellers. A skeg, or extended keel, may be incorporated at the stern to give good directional stability. The shape of the tug hull in plan view is also of great importance to the master of a vessel working in close proximity to ships and other floating objects. For many years the traditional tug was built with a very rounded stern to assist when going alongside or leaving a ship's side, allowing it to turn away easily. With modern tugs the use of twin screws and nozzles demands a stern shape that is less rounded to enable the steering gear to be accommodated and afford some protection to the propulsion equipment underwater. The eventual shape is almost certain to be a compromise between the need for some degree of roundness and the improved ability of a twin-screw vessel to manoeuvre at close quarters.

In larger sea-going vessels the underwater shape of the bow may be given a bulbous configuration in order to enhance the vessel's free running speed. The addition of a raised foredeck or a large fully enclosed forecastle is common in ship-handling tugs, which may be required to work in exposed locations and essential in larger sea-going vessels to combat the effects of heavy sea conditions.

The diagram shows, to scale, four different conventional screw vessels typical of those described in later pages. A tug/workboat of 16 metres long (below), a 27 metre twin screw harbour tug, a 64 metre anchor-handling tug and an anchor-handling oil rig supply vessel of 74 metres.

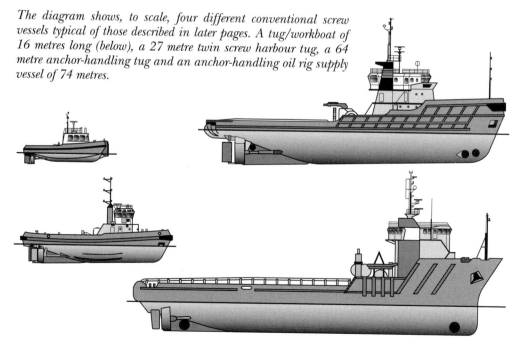

A transverse bow thrust unit is becoming an increasingly common feature in tugs of almost any size to improve handling when the vessel is manoeuvring. They are virtually indispensable in large tugs working in the offshore oil industry and in offshore supply vessels. In these vessels it is not uncommon to find transverse thrusters fitted at bow and stern.

Offshore supply vessels are invariably much longer than a normal seagoing or anchor-handling tug, and will have a significant cargo capacity. The cargo to be accommodated will generally require additional storage tanks, incorporated as part of the hull structure, and a large expanse of open deck for the transportation of containerised stores and drilling pipe to oil rigs. A hull form will be chosen that encompasses those needs. It must provide a good economical turn of speed, adequate towing characteristics and the ability to handle well when manoeuvring in close proximity to oil rigs and other offshore installations.

There are other vessels covered by this book, such as pusher tugs and multi-purpose work vessels, that also incorporate conventional screw propulsion. These generally have a comparatively simple, barge-like hull form. These and conventional tugs designed or adapted for pushing are described in more detail in later chapters.

Combi-tugs

There are a number of operators, mainly in Europe, that favour a ship-handling tug based on a conventional single-screw vessel but enhanced by the installation of a small azimuthing propulsion unit located beneath the bow. This arrangement improves the vessel's ability to manoeuvre considerably and provides a few tonnes (2 to 6) of additional bollard pull. Tugs equipped in this way are particularly useful for ship-handling work in dock systems and other confined spaces.

In most instances the vessels concerned are ones that have been modified by fitting the additional propulsion system at a later date. There are, however, examples of purpose-built combi-tugs being put into service in Europe as late as 1993. There is very little change required in the tug's structure, apart from providing accommodation for the propulsion unit and its associated power plant. A retractable thruster unit is the most common choice, with its machinery located in the forepeak and the steerable propeller extending through the hull plating when in use.

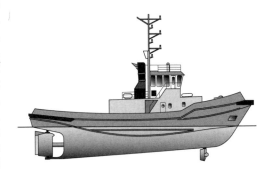

A "Combi" tug is a conventional single screw vessel fitted with a retractable azimuthing thruster unit beneath the bow. This example is a design introduced by the Belgian company U.R.S. in 1994.

Stern-drive tugs

The nearest relative to the conventional screw tug in hull design is the stern-drive vessel. This is a vessel where normal propellers and shafts have been replaced by azimuthing propulsion units, which enable the propeller and its associated nozzle

Portgarth is a "stern drive" tug built by Damen Shipyards to a standard design designated ASD 3110. She is a vessel of 262 gross tons, 30.7 metres in length, and 4049 bhp operated at Avonmouth by Cory Towage Ltd. *(Author)*

to be rotated (or steered) about a vertical axis. Such vessels are invariably fitted with a pair of propulsion units, located in approximately the same position as the propellers of a twin-screw tug. Each of the propulsion units is normally capable of being controlled independently, enabling thrust from each unit to be directed at any angle in relation to the hull. Manoeuvrability is improved dramatically when compared with a conventional screw tug. The vessel can be made to move forwards, backwards, sideways and turn in its own length with great precision in the hands of an experienced tug master.

Manoeuvrability, relatively high bollard pull performance and no significant increase in the draft of the vessel has made the stern-drive tug a viable alternative to tractor tugs in many applications. Tugs of the stern-drive type are sometimes referred to as "Reverse tractors". This term can and does cause confusion and has therefore been avoided in this book. Later chapters deal in more detail with azimuthing propulsion units, their controls and how tugs equipped in this way are employed.

The stern-drive configuration is most commonly found in powerful ship-handling tugs and is particularly popular in applications where power and manoeuvrability of a very high order are a prime requirement, such as tanker-handling vessels and escort tugs. Stern-drive vessels were first introduced in Japan and elsewhere in Asia, but in recent years have appeared in increasing numbers in the tug fleets of Europe and North America. In principle, the hull design used in tugs of this type differs very little from those employing conventional propellers. The main difference is that the underside of the stern must be of a suitable shape

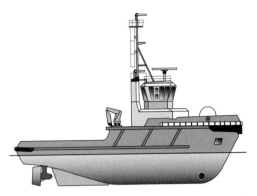

The diagram shows a "stern drive" tug typical of many being delivered to the towage industry in Europe in the mid 1990s. The configuration of the forward hull and the size of the skeg varies considerably between designs. This example incorporates a bow thrust unit.

to accept the propulsion unit mountings and have sufficient structural strength to accommodate loadings quite different from those imposed by a conventional propeller and rudder system. In most vessels the propulsion units are accessible through removable plates in the afterdeck, and may be lifted out vertically for repair.

In early stern-drive vessels the underwater shape of the hull was little different from that of a conventional screw tug, apart from the features previously mentioned. More recently there has been considerable research into the performance of this type of vessel used in the ship-handling and escorting role. Among the operational requirements expected of a powerful stern-drive tug is a good performance when going astern, and the ability to handle well when manoeuvring and towing in the indirect mode, that is when the tug's hull is being used to help control the tow. Naval architects have approached these needs in different ways, resulting in vessels with very similar specifications and performance but having quite different hull forms. The shape of the hull in the vicinity of the propulsion units is particularly important. Rotation of the units, with thrust produced in any direction, makes the need to maintain good water flow to the propellers a prime consideration in determining the underwater shape of the hull.

In most other respects the features of a stern-drive tug follow closely the rules that apply to a modern conventional screw tug. A raised foredeck is a feature frequently incorporated in tugs of this type, and a complete forecastle is employed in vessels intended to operate at sea or in exposed loca-tions. Stern-drive tugs employed in ship-handling work are invariably equipped with a towing winch on the

In a "stern drive" vessel the propulsion units are mounted in approximately the same position as the propellers of a conventional screw tug.

foredeck or forecastle and are therefore strengthened accordingly. Another common feature is the installation of a transverse bow thrust unit, to enhance manoeuvrability and station-keeping even further.

There is a very small number of unique vessels in use in the Far East that employ Voith Schneider cycloidal propulsion units, located at the stern in place of the more usual azimuthing type. At this time there is nothing to indicate that the use of such vessels is likely to grow or become universally accepted; they will not therefore be described here in any detail.

Voith Schneider tractor tugs

The introduction of the Voith Schneider tractor tug brought a whole new concept to the towing industry. The cycloidal propeller is a unique device, described in detail in Chapter 2, comprising a number of vertical blades that follow a circular orbit and produce thrust by means of their hydrodynamic profile and ability to change pitch at certain points in their circular path. Although this type of propulsion unit has many other applications, such as in ferries and other vessels where precise control is necessary, the combination of the cycloidal propeller and the tractor concept produced a tug that was to revolutionise towing for many operators. The term "tractor" is used where the propulsion units are located in the forward part of the vessel.

The Voith Schneider tractor tug was originally introduced for ship-handling work and became popular largely due to its exceptional manoeuvrability and safety in operation, inherent in the tractor principle. Early designs had the disadvantage of being relatively low-powered and employing cycloidal propulsion units that were less efficient than screw propellers of the time. Improvements in the size and performance of the Voith propulsion units and sophistication of tractor designs has resulted in the concept spreading from Europe, where it was quickly adopted by many towage companies, to fleets throughout the world. Tractor tugs of this type have grown in size and power to compete with vessels

Lady Josephine *is a Voith Schneider tractor tug of 364 gross tons and 4600 bhp built for Humber Tugs Ltd by McTay Marine in 1991. The vessel has a bollard pull of 56 tonnes and was built to a popular design with many advanced features.*   *(Author)*

employing other modern propulsion systems used in tanker-handling, escort and pollution-control work. At the time of writing Voith tractor tugs of 8,000 bhp and 47.24 metres (155 feet) in length are in service in this role.

The hull of a Voith Schneider tractor has a number of essential features. In a modern vessel two propulsion units are located beneath the hull of the tug about one third of its length from the bow. Earlier designs incorporated just one unit, but experience was soon to show that two such propellers, fitted side by side, dramatically improved the vessel's performance and agility. Another important feature is the large skeg, or vertical fin, located beneath the stern. The size and position of the skeg is critical, and is directly related to the position of the towing connection on the deck above. Located beneath the blades of the propulsion unit is a protection plate, held in position by a number of supporting struts. The protection plate has several functions: it affords some protection to the rotating blades when the vessel is working in shallow water, and provides a supporting structure when the tug is placed in dry dock or on a slipway for repairs. The performance of the propulsion units is also affected by the protection plate, which creates a nozzle effect in the water flow between the hull and plate with a resulting improvement in thrust.

In order to meet the constant demand for greater performance and as a result of the availability of more powerful engines, the size of propulsion units has increased considerably in recent years. This had resulted in the use of units with a blade orbit of well over 3 metres in diameter. To accommodate two such units, side by side, in the hull of a powerful ship-handling tug of perhaps 4,600 brake horsepower and 30 metres in length, demands a hull with considerable beam and volume. Very much larger vessels are now in service for specialist use, as escort tugs and rapid-response pollution-control vessels. The concept of the Voith tractor, combining the use of cycloidal propellers with the carefully developed hull configuration, is unique and gives vessels of this type an inherent ability to travel astern safely at relatively high speeds, push with the stern and tow in the indirect mode. The inherent ability to apply indirect towing methods, making full use of the vessel's large skeg, underwater shape and towing gear configuration, is

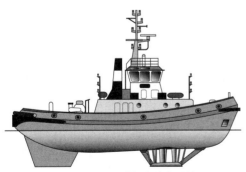

The diagram depicts a Voith Schneider tractor tug with a hull and superstructure design typical of many vessels used throughout Europe and elsewhere. Note the position of the propulsion units and skeg.

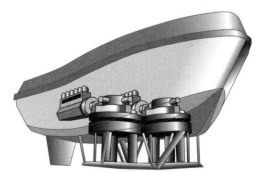

In the Voith Schneider tractor the propulsion units are mounted side by side above a "protection plate" and foward of the main engines.

a well-publicised feature of this type of vessel. This and the ability to operate in a true "push-pull" role is seen as a very great advantage by many operators, as will be seen in later chapters. A possible disadvantage is the vulnerability of the propulsion units, located beneath the hull, and the resulting increase in draught.

Very recent designs incorporate hull forms that are very close to that of a true "double-ended" vessel, with the enhanced ability to travel at high speed in either direction, yet able to carry out all the other functions required of a powerful ship-handling tug. The hull structure of a Voith tractor, as one would expect, incorporates many of the same features common in tugs of all types. A suitable raised foredeck or forecastle is incorporated where necessary. In plan view the hull is invariably well rounded to give a sympathetic shape for working in close proximity with ships, but the stern structure is frequently designed to provide a broad fendered area for pushing. A strengthened bow with extensive fendering is rarely necessary.

Tractor tugs with azimuthing propulsion units

Tractor tugs employing propulsion units of the azimuthing type, using steerable screw propellers, were first built in Europe in the early 1970s as a possible alternative to the Voith Schneider system, introduced some years earlier. The units are mounted in much the same way, side by side, under the forward part of the hull. With the exception of a few very small vessels used in the logging industry, the units are always fitted in pairs. Tugs of this type are designed to perform in much the same way as their Voith Schneider counterparts, but may be less suitable for towing in the indirect mode. Early vessels often had the advantage of improved performance (in terms of horsepower per tonne bollard pull) due to

The azimuthing tractor tug Z P Montelena *is a vessel of 198 gross tons and 29.19 metres in length with a bollard pull of 53 tonnes, originally built for use in the USA in 1983. The 3340 bhp vessel is now operated by KOTUG in Rotterdam.* (Author)

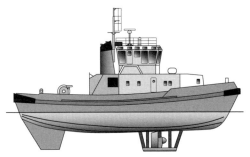

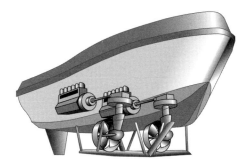

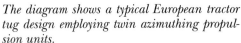

The diagram shows a typical European tractor tug design employing twin azimuthing propulsion units.

The configuration of an azimuthing tractor showing the position of the engines, propulsion units and a typical protection plate.

their use of azimuthing propulsion units embodying more efficient screw propellers and reduced capital cost. More recently the development of larger and more powerful Voith Schneider cycloidal propellers has tended to nullify this advantage. For this reason, and the growing popularity of stern-drive vessels, the development of tractor tugs with azimuthing units has slowed noticeably.

The hull configuration incorporates a fixed skeg and a form of protection plate, similar to that of the Voith tractor. Protection plate design varies from a device fitted solely to protect the units and assist with docking, to a more comprehensive structure intended to improve propulsion unit performance. A feature of some modern tractors of this type is the location of the propulsion units in a shallow recess or tunnel beneath the hull in order to reduce the draught of the vessel. With this arrangement it is necessary to ensure that the effectiveness of the units is not seriously impaired by restricted water flow to the propellers.

Special features of tug hull design
The hull design of virtually any tug will have a number of features that are less common in ships of other types or have particular significance in the towage industry. Some of the more important items are described below.

Anchors and anchor pockets
Anchors are fitted to most tugs of any size, either for use in an emergency or to enable the vessel to go to anchor as part of its normal operation, as with any other ship. In sea-going vessels above a given size anchors are a mandatory requirement. The type and number of anchors required may vary with the country and regulatory authorities concerned. It is the stowage of anchors when they are not in use that often gives cause for concern among tug operators, particularly in ship-handling vessels and those operating in close proximity to other craft. By its nature an anchor is an unwieldy object, difficult to stow and capable of doing considerable damage if unrestrained. If the anchors are located in the bow, which is normal in the vast majority of tugs and oil rig supply vessels, they are stowed in recesses in the hull shell plating often known as a pocket. When the anchor is raised it is hauled into the pocket with little or nothing to protrude and possibly cause damage to other vessels or fouling of ropes.

In some harbour tugs only one anchor is required for occasional or emergency use. Where this is the case it is located in the bow or in a pocket beneath the stern. The latter arrangement is particularly popular in tractor tugs where the propulsion units are located in the forepart of the vessel and well away from the anchor and its chain. The anchors are handled either by a separate anchor windlass or by part of the towing winch mechanism. Modern stern-drive vessels, with a large towing winch on the foredeck, invariably use the latter arrangement. The controls for the anchor windlass are now frequently located in the wheelhouse in easy reach of the tug master.

Bulwarks

The side plating above deck level forming a protective barrier around the main working decks of the vessel is known as the bulwarks. The bulwarks of a tug are generally of much heavier construction than those found in other ships and are intended to provide protection from the sea and water coming on deck when working alongside other moving vessels. They also provide some physical security for personnel working on deck under difficult conditions. The height of bulwarks varies with the type of vessel and its employment, but is subject to national

This view of the stern drive tug Portgarth *shows clearly the inset bulwarks and other features designed to give clearance when alongside ships. Note also the carefully designed fendering, forward towing winch and fairlead.* *(Author)*

regulations. Large tugs, including some ship-handling vessels, have hinged access doors on one or both sides of the tug to enable personnel to move safely from one vessel to another without climbing high bulwarks. Similar openings may be incorporated to allow anti-pollution equipment to be deployed, divers to be put in the water and maintenance tasks to be carried out on buoys or floating pipelines. An open stern, totally devoid of bulwarks, is a common feature in anchor-handling vessels and those engaged in pollution-control work.

Small tugs working on inland waterways may have very low bulwarks, or sections where the height is reduced, in order to prevent fouling or chafing towing gear. The bulwarks of all tugs have openings or freeing devices to ensure that any water taken on deck drains quickly overboard. In most tug designs the bulwarks slope in from deck level to the top rail, particularly around the stern and sides of the vessel; this is sometimes known as the "tumble home" and is intended to reduce the possibility of contact damage when the tug rolls while alongside another vessel. A similar remedy is to position the bulwarks in from the deck edge by up to half a metre (see also the following section on Superstructure design).

Decks
The working areas on the towing decks and afterdecks of tugs and oil rig supply vessels are worthy of mention. These areas are frequently wet, taking a small amount of water on board when the vessel heels over while towing, and susceptible to flooding in heavy weather. They remain, however, areas where men must continue to work under the most difficult conditions. A non-skid surface, of special paint or compound, is normally applied to all exposed working decks. In the case of anchor-handling tugs and vessels engaged in similar work, where heavy anchors, buoys, pipeline components and the like are hauled on board through an open stern, a heavy timber sheathing is fitted over the working area to protect the deck from structural damage and provide a more suitable surface on which to handle these items. When the timber becomes seriously damaged it is easily replaced.

Fendering
One of the most distinctive features of almost any tug are the fenders used to protect the vessel from damage when it is working in close proximity to other vessels. Most forms of towing must be regarded as a "contact sport" where direct contact with the vessel being assisted is either essential or unavoidable. Throughout its history the towage industry has worked hard to find a suitable shock-absorbing medium to cushion the interface between tug and tow. In modern tugs a great deal of effort has gone into developing moulded rubber fendering and the structures needed to satisfactorily mount it on the tug. The resulting designs must be capable of absorbing the vast amounts of energy generated when two sizeable vessels repeatedly make contact with each other. This fendering not only has to protect the vessel from unavoidable impact damage but must also survive the considerable abrasion encountered in towing operations.

In high-powered ship-handling tugs the question of effective fendering is complex. The problem is not just a simple one of impact absorption; there is also a need to distribute the force effectively when the tug is pushing on a ship. There have been many examples of damage to the hull plating of tankers and other ships, hence the need to distribute the force over a reasonably wide area. Abrasion caused when the tug ranges up and down against another vessel in a swell may also have serious consequences for the life of the fender and its mountings. To combat this phenomenon some operators incorporate a water spray system to lubricate rubber bow or stern fenders when the tug is pushing. Others argue that some adhesion is essential to ensure that the tug can be held in position on the side of a ship under these circumstances. Among the various solutions produced by designers are substantial tubular rubber fenders that completely encircle the tug, fenders made from complex rubber mouldings to fit specific parts of the vessel, and examples fabricated from rubber sections to form complete bow or stern fenders.

In spite of the effort put into the design of suitable fendering systems, there remains a place for the humble motor tyre, which has for so long been such an obvious appendage on tugs of all types. It is still quite common to see modern rubber fendering given the secondary protection of a layer of tyres. Discarded tyres from trucks, earthmoving vehicles and especially aircraft remain extremely effective in this role. Tyres used in this way are generally secured to the vessel's bulwarks by means of chains or steel wire strops. Fenders manufactured from rope were a traditional remedy employed by tug companies around the world for many decades as a substitute for, or in addition to, rubber fendering. This form of fender lacks the resilience of rubber and is therefore less suited to the high forces involved in modern tug operation, but is still used in some companies as secondary protection. In the past, rotating bow fenders have been used incorporating very heavy automotive wheels complete with inflated tyres and disc brakes to control rotation. These now appear to be less prevalent, but the use of two or more tyres mounted on a vertical pillar to form a bow fender continues to be popular in some North American tugs.

Tugs used for special purposes may have additional fendering. Those employed in naval yards to assist submarines, for example, are fitted with fenders that extend well below the waterline. In this way the tug may work close to the partly submerged pressure hull of a submarine without fear of causing damage. Deep-sea tugs and oil rig supply vessels have less need for bow fenders, but may be heavily strengthened around the stern and sides. This takes the form of heavy steel rubbing strakes, often faced with rubber or again overlaid with heavy vehicle tyres.

Forecastles and raised foredecks

The purpose of incorporating a forecastle in a tug of any size is to improve its ability to work at sea or in exposed waters. By raising the deck at the bow improvements can be made to the shape of the forward hull, reducing the likelihood of the vessel taking water on board when it encounters heavy seas or is operating in a swell. This improves the handling of the tug and provides a safer, drier environment for those working on deck. It is common for the forecastle to be one whole deck higher than the main, or towing, deck, enabling the space gained to be used for accommodation or additional machinery.

Cramond *is one of two 4800 bhp tankers handling stern drive tugs employed by British Petroleum at their Hound Point terminal in Scotland. Clearly visible is the high forecastle, well glazed wheelhouse and exhaust uptakes positioned for clearance. Note also the open stern and clear afterdeck.* (Author)

Smaller tugs, designed to work in more sheltered conditions, may be given a raised foredeck. This compromise gives the crew ready access when moving from one end of the vessel to the other, but still affords some protection. The raised area may take the form of a steeply sloping deck or a foredeck raised by a metre or so.

Watertight compartments and subdivisions
The hull of almost any vessel, from a small boat to a huge cargo ship, generally incorporates some means of subdividing the hull into a number of watertight compartments in order to minimise the danger of sinking if an accident occurs. A tug hull is treated in similar fashion, but the problem of providing watertight compartments of a suitable size, due to the very large size of the engine room in relation the rest of the hull, is particularly difficult in many vessels such as ship-handling tugs. Any accident resulting in the penetration of the external hull plating in the engine room area, or flooding of that compartment from any other cause, will seriously affect the vessel's ability to stay afloat. Many tugs have been lost through contact damage or capsizing, causing the engine room to flood and the vessel to sink very quickly indeed.

There are several features that are often incorporated in the hull of a tug to improve the safety of the vessel in this respect. One common remedy is to ensure that fuel, oil, ballast and other storage tanks are located in the bottom and sides of the hull, reducing the areas where direct penetration of the large machinery spaces can occur. In the case of a tractor tug or stern-drive vessel, the total volume of the combined machinery space can be enormous. This situation is sometimes improved by placing a transverse watertight bulkhead between the engines and the propulsion unit space, but the need to seal the apertures where the rotating drive shafts pass through can present problems. Likewise, self-contained auxiliary machinery such as generators and pumps may be located in separate compartments. Carefully positioned storerooms and workshop areas are often fitted with watertight doors to afford additional buoyancy in the event of an emergency.

Superstructure design
In the past a ready means of identification between various vessels has been the design of a tug's superstructure. The size, shape and position of the wheelhouse, upperworks, funnels or exhaust uptakes has been a major clue as to the type of vessel, and often the part of the world it has come from. The most pronounced regional difference is that between European and American tugs. In conventional screw vessels, European tugs invariably have a long afterdeck with the towing connection made at a point very close to amidships. In North America early regulations governing crew accommodation resulted in the very long deckhouses so characteristic of American vessels, and a towing connection much nearer the stern. To some extent these assumptions remain true, but modern tractor and stern-drive vessels, by their nature, have tended to introduce greater commonality. The application of new propulsion systems and towing methods has imposed certain design constraints on particular types of vessel, whether produced in America, Japan or Europe. In terms of superstructure design, a tug is unique among vessels and has quite different priorities where visibility, safety of operation and crew accommodation are concerned. Some of the more important considerations are described in the following paragraphs.

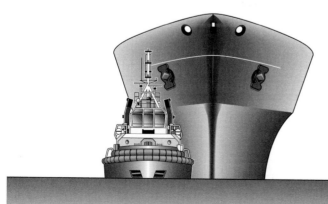

The superstructure and bulwarks of ship-handling tugs are designed to minimise damage when the vessel works close alongside ships with flared bows or over-hanging sterns.

Clearance

The overall "shape" of the superstructure is of prime importance if the tug is to work safely and efficiently. Almost every tug is required to work close alongside other vessels of one sort or another, often ships very much larger than the tug itself. It is therefore necessary to ensure that no part of the tug's structure will make contact with the other vessel, particularly in conditions when either vessel rolls in heavy weather conditions or when the tug heels over while towing or pushing. To ensure that there is sufficient clearance under these circumstances the various portions of the superstructure are narrowed or "set in" as shown in the accompanying diagram. As previously mentioned, the bulwarks are similarly arranged to prevent contact damage. A profile that is designed to give adequate clearance often has the advantage of good lines of sight from the wheelhouse to the various working areas around the tug.

The wheelhouse

The wheelhouse is the centre of operations on every modern tug. It is from here that the tug captain must effectively control the vessel and much of her equipment while towing and carrying out the tug's various duties. Remotely operated controls and a wide range of navigational and other aids enable many functions to be carried out by the master that would once have been carried out by crew members on deck or in the engine room. As mentioned in later chapters,

The tractor tug Redbridge, *built in 1995 for Red Funnel Tugs of Southampton, incorporates exhaust stacks and a wheelhouse designed to afford the best possible visibility for the tug master when operating stern first. All crew accommodation is above deck level.* (Author)

controls for the engines, propulsion system and much of the deck equipment are now located in the wheelhouse. Other equipment is provided for the safe navigation of the tug and to enable her to communicate with other shipping, her owners, port authorities and agents. For much of the time the wheelhouses of many smaller tugs may be occupied by just one man, and considerable effort has gone into ensuring that controls and equipment are readily accessible and can be operated comfortably.

It is around this working environment that the wheelhouse is configured, and one of the most important considerations is good all-round visibility. The majority of tugs spend their working lives operating in very close proximity to other vessels, and for much of the time the tug master is preoccupied with events happening astern of him or immediately alongside. In order to provide the best possible all-round vision, wheelhouse designs have changed dramatically, from a simple rectangular structure at the forward end of the superstructure, to a prominent, glazed control position with clear all-round visibility. Wheelhouse windows are generally angled forward at the top and may also be tinted to reduce glare in bright conditions and reflections at night.

It is not only essential to have good vision around the vessel, but also overhead. When ship-handling tugs are at work beneath the overhanging bow or stern of a large ship, the tug master must be able to see what is happening above him, particularly when the towing connection is being made. Likewise the master of an anchor-handling tug will often operate in a similar fashion adjacent to oil rigs and other offshore structures. To meet this need the wheelhouses of most modern tugs are fitted with sloping windows around the periphery of the roof. In larger vessels the controls for the propulsion system, winches and other deck equipment may be duplicated on either side of the wheelhouse, and if necessary at the rear, overlooking the stern. A stern-facing control position is common in anchor-handling tugs and oil rig supply vessels where much of the vessel's work is carried out on the afterdeck.

Accommodation

The accommodation provided aboard a modern tug is generally of a very high standard, but the size and scope of facilities provided depends largely on the type of vessel and her employment. At one end of the scale a small tug used mainly for harbour duties, and manned only for short periods, may only require very simple domestic facilities and very little sleeping accommodation. Conversely, a large deep-sea tug or supply vessel will have a crew of a dozen or so and be equipped to provide all their needs on voyages lasting several weeks, in a variety of climatic conditions. Between these extreme examples are a wide variety of needs met by individual operators when vessels are fitted out. The actual location and basic standard of accommodation is strictly regulated by the various maritime authorities and classification societies. In later vessels living accommodation is invariably located above the waterline for safety reasons, and certain standards have to be met regarding access and emergency escape routes. The use of high-speed diesel engines and modern propulsion systems has increased the need to isolate living accommodation from the effects of noise and vibration by the extensive use of insulation material. In some cases the accommodation is located above the waterline or main deck level and isolated from the main hull structure by special anti-vibration mountings.

Where sleeping accommodation is required for regular use in modern vessels, a cabin is normally available for each crew member, and rarely do more than two men have to share. Provision is also made for the preparation of food, dry and refrigerated storage, showers or bathing and laundering clothes. Adequate facilities are also required for the important matter of drying and storing the foul weather clothing used by personnel working on deck in all weather conditions. Very large vessels will have additional accommodation for owner's staff, salvage personnel, divers and running crews (the last-mentioned term refers to the additional personnel required to man ships or similar vessels in tow). Air conditioning systems are an essential requirement in tugs built for use in tropical regions and in vessels designed for long-distance towing, which may encounter a whole variety of climatic conditions. The increased use of tugs and oil rig supply vessels in sub-zero temperatures calls not only for comprehensive heating systems to be installed for accommodation and domestic use, but also that all of the tug's machinery systems, on deck and elsewhere, remain operational and free of ice.

As with the hull, certain aspects of the superstructure can also affect the watertight integrity of the vessel. Doors, windows and portholes must all be capable of remaining watertight in the environment in which the vessel will be expected to work. Sea-going vessels will have steel doors that can be sealed when conditions dictate. In some vessels regulations also require a watertight door or hatch to be fitted between the wheelhouse and the rest of the superstructure.

Smit-Lloyd 56 is typical of many powerful anchor-handling oil rig supply vessels. Her wheelhouse and the position of her exhaust uptakes is designed to give good all round vision. A high standard of accommodation is incorporated in the superstructure and forecastle. The vessel is twin screw with two bow and one stern thruster. (Author)

This is to prevent serious flooding should the wheelhouse windows be broken by heavy seas, a rare but very real possibility.

Funnels and exhaust stacks
The continuing use of funnels has been an emotive subject in some tug companies for very many years. Since the demise of steam-powered vessels the need for a large, prominent funnel of the traditional type has largely disappeared. However, the funnel provides a convenient surface for the operators to display their liveries, and acts as a ready means of identification, a factor still firmly in the minds of some owners. A major disadvantage of the traditional funnel, or even its streamlined successor, is that it invariably interferes with the all-round vision required from the wheelhouse. The need to carry exhaust fumes away from the vessel remains a very real problem that has been tackled in many different ways. Exhaust outlets in the hull, usually in the stern, are not uncommon, but in tugs of any size a high-level outlet is generally preferred to ensure that personnel working on deck are not affected by noxious fumes. In most cases one or two slim vertical uptakes are used and located in a position designed to minimise the effect on all-round vision. This has resulted in small offset funnels, single unclad exhaust pipes and a multitude of other uptake designs, positioned in a variety of ways. Some tractor tugs now have funnels or uptakes positioned in front of the wheelhouse on the premise that maximum visibility is required over the stern.

Tug building
The companies most frequently involved in the construction of tugs are those in the business of producing small specialist ships incorporating a high level of modern technology. Gone are the days when a whole host of shipbuilders were available to build vessels of any type using traditional shipbuilding methods. As the shipbuilding industry has decreased in size worldwide, specialist shipyards have emerged to undertake vessels of a particular type. The shipyards that remain have been forced to adopt modern manufacturing methods in order to survive in a highly competitive worldwide market.

The design
When a tug is ordered the design work will be undertaken by the owner, an independent consultant, or the design department of the shipyard concerned; often a mix of all three will be used to achieve the result required by a particular owner. In these days of advanced propulsion technology, significant input may also come from the manufacturer of the propulsion system, some of whom carry out extensive research and testing to offer designs tailored to suit their particular propulsion equipment and aimed at a particular aspect of the towage market. To undertake the construction of a new vessel is a major and extremely expensive project for any tug owner. For example, the cost of building a "state of the art" ship-handling tug in Britain in 1995 was approximately £3–4 million (sterling). Mistakes made in specifying and designing a new vessel can therefore be expensive, so considerable effort goes into ensuring that the design will meet the owner's needs exactly.

The new tug Melton *is one of three "state of the art" stern drive, shiphandling tugs completed for Howard Smith Towage during 1996. 32.72 metres in length and 4819 bhp, the vessel's design incorporates many features intended to afford excellent all round vision and handling characteristics.* Melton *is seen arriving in Holland for fitting out at the Damen Shipyard. The hull and all major steelwork was constructed in Poland.* (R & F van der Hoek)

Marine architects and design consultants now rely heavily on computer simulation to test tug designs and establish the best possible methods of handling ships or other towage operations. Programmes that can simulate tidal conditions, wind, a ship's handling characteristics and the power and position of tugs required to carry out a particular operation are now in regular use. From these studies considerable information can be established about the type of vessel required before an order is placed. This is particularly valuable if the operating environment or vessels to be handled are new and historical operating data is not available. If a completely new vessel is contemplated the hull form will be tested using scale models in a special test tank facility. Tank testing with models provides data on how the new vessel will handle, and its stability, performance and sea-going characteristics. The information obtained from such tests may well be used to provide data for computer modelling and simulation. Once the basic configuration has been decided, a Computer Aided Design (CAD) system may be used to produce the general arrangement and detailed drawings that will eventually be necessary for the shipyard to proceed with construction. The strength of the vessel is particularly important in the design of a tug. Because of the work that they do, tugs of all sizes need to be rugged to withstand external forces on the hull and forces generated by the use of high-powered propulsion machinery, well above those experienced by cargo or passenger vessels. A tug must be capable of withstanding the rigours of working alongside other vessels and often the possibility of being "squeezed" between barges or perhaps a ship and a quay wall. To avoid the possibility of serious damage, such considerations are taken into account in the design process. The strength of a tug's hull is largely determined by the thickness of the external plates, and the spacing and size of internal frames and bulkhead; the broad and ancient term "scantlings" is frequently used in ship construction to describe these features. Internally, the hull structure may be quite complex, particularly in the stern area where additional strength is achieved by carefully designed longitudinal and transverse stiffening. Much of the work of predicting the necessary structural strength and determining the design of the final structure will be carried out using the CAD system. Stress calculations that took many hours a few years ago are completed almost instantly by a computer. Likewise, critical calculations concerning the

The stern section of a twin screw tug under construction, upside down, in the building hall of Damen Shipyard of Gorinchem in Holland. *(Damen Shipyard)*

finished vessel's stability in its various operating modes will be done using the computer system.

In some instances a sophisticated CAD system may have the ability to assist the owner and designer by showing graphically the effects of changes in the size and position of structures, equipment and accommodation. This is a considerable help in assessing, for example, the all-round visibility from various positions in the wheelhouse, checking that legal requirements are met for stability and accommodation, or simply validating the routes for pipework, etc. A great deal of thought is given to the positioning of the various controls and other pieces of equipment in the wheelhouse, to achieve a sound operating layout. This too may be simulated by computer modelling, but a full-scale "mock-up" is sometimes constructed in wood to evaluate the final design. When the design process is finished, general arrangement and individual component drawings are produced for the shipyard, and work on the vessel can start.

The building process
A tug's hull is almost invariably a welded steel structure. In the majority of cases steel is also used in the superstructure and for other major items incorporated in the vessel's construction. Aluminium alloy is sometimes used in the construction of the superstructure to reduce weight, but rarely in the hull, and then only in very small vessels. The steel plate used in construction is frequently cleaned and

Three tugs destined for use in the Arabian Gulf being fitted out and painted indoors at Damen Shipyard. (Author)

primed for painting when it arrives in the shipyard to reduce the growth of rust during the construction process. Alternatively, the finished structure will be shot-blasted and primed at an early stage.

In a modern shipyard the steel plates for the main structure will be cut by a computer-controlled machine using plasma arc or gas cutting equipment. The cutting machine may utilise information derived from the CAD system to produce accurate results with very little waste material. Component parts produced in this way fit accurately together ready for welding, often by a semi-automated electric arc welding machine. Many modern shipyards have the ability to construct either the whole vessel or large parts of the structure undercover in huge workshops or covered dry docks. This has the advantage of ensuring that work continues unaffected by bad weather, and reduces the adverse effects of rain on the partly built structure. Both of these considerations have favourable economic connotations. The main components of the hull and superstructure are frequently built up in "blocks" and welded together as construction proceeds. To speed up the process some of these component parts may be sub-contracted to other shipyards or steel fabrication specialists. Economic considerations may involve the construction of complete hulls by yards located in areas where favourable labour rates prevail or international monetary exchange rates render some financial advantage. This has proved particularly relevant in the case of series-built vessels where large numbers of similar craft may be involved.

Series construction gives some economic advantages, particularly in the production of small vessels. Three small line handling tugs are shown prior to launching at the shipyard of McTay Marine of Bromborough. *(McTay Marine)*

This view of the Damen Shipyard at Gorinchem dramatically illustrates the philosophy of series production. Over fifty "stock" hulls and partly completed tugs of all sizes are visible in this aerial photograph. *(Damen Shipyard)*

Standard tugs and series production

No account of tug building would be complete without further mention of the advantages of series production and the use of standard designs. Tugs have always, because of the relatively small size, lent themselves to production in large numbers with the economic benefits that result. This was amply demonstrated during both World Wars when large numbers of tugs and other small vessels were constructed cheaply in a very short time. More recently there has been a tendency for tug owners to build new vessels in small numbers, of two or more, in order to gain some financial advantage and achieve some commonality to aid maintenance and operation. A number of specialist shipbuilders in Europe, the USA and Asia have exploited these advantages vigorously and offer owners standard designs ranging from very small tug/workboats to large and sophisticated oil rig supply vessels. Tug builders in Holland, originally responsible for the introduction of small, mass-produced tugs now provide vessels of all types and sizes to owners all round the world.

The standard designs offered by specialist builders are widely researched and intended to satisfy the needs of a large cross-section of operators. Using basic standard hull designs, usually identified by overall length and propulsion configuration, owners are given a choice of engines and equipment. Deviations from the standard design can be made, but will adversely affect the final cost. A major advantage of adopting a standard tug design is the possibility of an incredibly quick delivery of the finished vessel. Large specialist companies often carry a stock of standard hulls that can be fitted out and completed to an owner's specification in a very short time. Similar stocks are maintained of other standard components, engines and propulsion equipment, with the further advantage that a ready source of spare parts will be available at a later date.

Launching and fitting out
With relatively small ships such as tugs, the vessel will be almost complete when it is put into the water. In the past the hull would have been launched as soon as the main structure was complete, and the machinery installed afterwards. More recently it has become common practice to install virtually all of the major machinery components while the vessel is still on dry land. If the vessel is built under cover it is usual for the maximum amount of work to be completed while it is still unaffected by weather, including much of the detailed fitting out in the accommodation and engine room. Whatever the facilities available, the tug still has to be launched by one means or another. Traditional launchings, where the vessel enters the water stern-first or sideways, making a spectacular splash, are becoming less common. More often than not the partially completed tug will be moved from the construction shed to a slipway or lift and lowered gently into the water. In some yards, where vessels are built in a covered dry dock, the dock is flooded and the tug floated out. Smaller craft may be lifted into the water by crane. However the vessel is launched, there are various tasks that cannot be

The Voith Schneider tractor tug Fidra, *under construction for the Forth Ports Authority, has been moved to the bottom of the slipway at McTay Marine ready to be floated off at high tide. All items of main machinery are in place and fitting out is at an advanced stage.* (Author)

undertaken until it is in the water. A major consideration is the final lining-up of engines, gearboxes, propulsion units and other major items of machinery. This important work is not generally carried out until the tug is afloat and the hull is supported by the water, due to the possibility of minute structural changes taking place during the launching process. A representative of the owners, usually a senior member of the company's engineering staff or the chief engineer designated to serve on the new vessel, will be constantly in attendance at the shipyard during the final stages of construction and the fitting-out process. This ensures that decisions regarding minor changes and quality standards can be made without undue delay, and that the owner's staff rapidly become familiar with their new equipment.

As previously mentioned, the amount of fitting-out work still to be done will vary, often depending on the facilities available at the site where the hull was constructed. Whatever the level of completion, the remaining work to finish and equip the vessel will be done afloat in the yard's fitting-out berth. Electrical wiring will be completed and the installation of navigational aids carried out. Much of this equipment is frequently hired or leased by tug owners and will be installed by the supplier or a specialist fairly late in the fitting-out process. The matter of painting is also worthy of mention. In the present financial climate the paint finish on a new vessel is an important factor, taken very seriously by most owners. A new tug will be painted with great care, using advanced paint and protective finish technology, not only to ensure that it will look good when delivered, but also to reduce the need for maintenance in the long term. With reduced manning levels and improved utilisation the crew of a modern tug have much less time to spend on a repainting than did their predecessors. Prior to launch the hull will have been treated below the waterline with an anti-fouling treatment that is impervious to the corrosive action of sea water and will resist the accumulation of marine growth, which quickly affects a vessel's performance. The superstructure and decks will be painted appropriately and attention will be given to the paint finish throughout the trials and pre-delivery period.

Trials
Before the new tug is delivered it is subjected to exhaustive trials to ensure that it does actually meet the owner's specification. The trials are normally conducted by the shipbuilder and attended by representatives from the owner, design consultants and specialists from the engine and propulsion equipment suppliers. Such trials cover not only the performance of the propulsion and steering systems, but also many other aspects of the vessel and her equipment. Tests are carried out to ensure that the deck machinery, fire-fighting installations, life-saving equipment and a whole host of other systems are operating correctly. Basin trials will be conducted, with the tug still at its moorings, to check that the engines and propulsion machinery operate correctly and react properly to the controls in the wheelhouse.

One of the trials to be carried out before the tug leaves the quay is likely to be an inclining test, to check that the vessel's stability characteristics are within the expected parameters. This is done by moving large weights, of known values, from one side of the vessel to the other and recording various measurements to

Ngan Chau *of the Hong Kong Salvage & Towage Co. Ltd. is seen here displaying her agility by turning in her own length. During trials the handling characteristics of all new vessels are fully tested.* Ngan Chau *is a 4000 bhp stern drive vessel of 456 gross tons built in 1994 for berthing and seagoing duties.* (Hong Kong S & T)

enable the centre of balance (known as GM) to be calculated. The GM is related to the vessel's "metacentric height" and is affected by draught, the vessel's loading, weight distribution and other variables. The whole question of stability is a particularly serious and complex matter in tug design and beyond the scope of this book.

Trials to confirm the handling characteristics of the new vessel will vary with the type of tug and the work that it is designed to do. Tests will be carried out to measure the tug's turning circle, going ahead and astern, response to varying degrees of helm, and stopping distances from different speeds. All control systems have an inherent time delay; these response times are important, particularly in ship-handling vessels, and are the subject of a great deal of attention during trials. From the bystander's point of view the "crash stop" is the most spectacular test. The vessel is brought to a stop from full speed by instantly going full astern. Any undesirable deviation from a satisfactory course during this procedure may be cause for concern. Tugs built to undertake other duties such as fire-fighting, pollution-control work, anchor-handling and perhaps pushing will all have specific trials carried out to confirm that those roles can be satisfactorily carried out safely and efficiently.

A bollard pull trial is an essential part of the pre-delivery performance testing carried out with all new tugs. Redbridge *has her towline secured to a dockside bollard. An electronic "load cell" is coupled into the connection and wired to recording equipment (inset).*   *(Author)*

The free running speed of a tug is measured in the time-honoured fashion using a measured mile. A number of runs are made over the measured distance, in each direction, to compensate for wind and tidal conditions. With some vessels the speed achieved when running astern is also important, and is measured in exactly the same way. The results are a calculated average speed expressed in knots.

Bollard pull trials

Last and by no means least is the bollard pull trial. The bollard pull rating for a vessel has become an important factor, and in many cases the one most likely to be scrutinised by a potential client. Due to the variety of propulsion systems now in use, it is no longer possible to judge the power of a tug by the horsepower of its engines alone. Therefore it has become necessary to adopt a bollard pull test that can be universally accepted as a measure of a vessel's ability to tow. Bollard pull is simply the amount of static pull the vessel can exert when tethered to a measuring device. The figure obtained is usually expressed in tonnes.

Bollard pull trials are normally conducted under strict conditions laid down by the classification society or authority that will ultimately certify the results. These conditions include specific requirements concerning the location for the trial and the condition of the vessel. One of the most important factors is the location. A large stretch of water is required, unaffected by tides and of suitable depth; the latter can be critical, especially in the case of powerful deep-draught tugs, the performance of which is affected by a phenomenon known as "ground effect". A depth of water of not less than 20 metres is typical, but not always easy to achieve at a suitable site. A bollard of adequate strength and proportions is also essential. A modern harbour tug will often produce a bollard pull of over 50 tonnes, and a very powerful tug supply vessel over 150 tonnes. It has been known for a dockside mooring bollard to be pulled bodily from its foundations during such a trial.

The tug's towline is shackled to the bollard with a measuring device inserted in the line. For many years a mechanical device, in the form of a very large spring balance known as a "clock", was used. Latterly modern electronic "load cell" devices have become more popular, and have the advantage of being lighter and capable of producing a graphical record and tables of results automatically. It is also possible to monitor the results remotely, either ashore or on board the vessel under test. The towline length is also a critical factor. A minimum length of 300 metres is typical, to avoid the adverse effects of water impinging upon dock walls. With the tug pulling against the measuring device in this way, readings are taken at various predetermined power settings for set periods of time. The most important result will be the maximum steady bollard pull achieved with the engines at their maximum continuous power setting. In most cases, particularly with ship-handling tugs, the trials will include the vessel pulling both ahead and astern, the astern pull being equally important in many applications. From the readings obtained tables of results are compiled for analysis.

CHAPTER 2

Propulsion
systems

The heart of every tug and the feature that probably attracts most attention is the propulsion system and engine. As we have seen in the previous chapter a wide choice of propulsion systems is available to the operator of a modern tug fleet. The most common options range from a single conventional screw propeller to highly sophisticated propulsion units intended to combine great pulling power with exceptional manoeuvrability and precise control.

This chapter describes in more detail the main systems mentioned, along with the basic types of tug, in Chapter 1. Engines are generally compatible with a wide range of propulsion systems and some of the propulsion equipment described here is used in more than one type of vessel or configured in a different manner. The control systems favoured by various manufacturers and owners also vary widely. Therefore examples have been chosen to give the simplest explanation of what are often quite complex systems. The operation of the different types of vessel will be dealt with in later chapters.

The main engine
The term "main engine" is used in marine circles to differentiate between an engine used to drive the main propulsion system and engines installed to provide power for other purposes, eg power generation, pumping, and driving other auxiliary equipment. In modern tugs diesel engines are invariably chosen as the means of providing power for both propulsion and auxiliary use. Whatever the choice of propulsion system – conventional propeller, azimuthing propulsion unit or Voith Schneider cycloidal propeller – the main engine will remain basically the same, and a type will be chosen to satisfy requirements such as power output, suitable operating speed ranges, power-to-weight ratio, fuel consumption and, increasingly, the ability to meet environmental regulations.

Since the diesel engine was first used in tugs, prior to the Second World War, the approach to its use has changed considerably. The large, slow-running diesel engines, coupled directly to the propeller shaft, popular for several decades are disappearing rapidly. A most noticeable feature of the modern tug's engine room is the relatively small size of the engines. Not only are engines smaller, they are very much more powerful for their size. Engines have been

One of two Stork Warsila 9F240 main engines installed in the stern drive tug Portgarth. *The 9 cylinder turbo-charged diesel is rated at 2025 brake horsepower (1490 Kw) at 1000 revs/minute.*
(Author)

developed to produce greater power by adding more cylinders and allowing them to run at much higher revolutions. This has been made possible by the use of modern designs, improved materials, and careful choice of cylinder configuration. There is stiff competition among rival manufacturers of marine engines to meet the demands of their customers in a cost-effective manner. As particular engines meet the needs of the towage industry at a given time they tend to become "fashionable" for a number of years, in certain geographical regions, until superseded by another.

A typical modern diesel engine, used widely by the European towage industry in a ship-handling tug, will be turbocharged and have six to eight cylinders arranged in line. A common example will produce in the order of 2,000–2,400 bhp at approximately 900/1,000 rpm. The rating of such engines will vary with the installation and the propulsion system, different maximum speeds giving different horsepower figures. Larger engines, producing much more power, may share common components with smaller engines from the same manufacturer's range. For example, a 12-cylinder engine, with its cylinders arranged in a "vee" formation, is likely to have many components in common with similar six- or eight-cylinder engines. Such commonality is practised throughout the world, as is the adoption of engines of a given type by various companies and fleets. There are benefits in this approach for the operator: the purchase and holding of spare parts is simplified and becomes more economical, and engineering staff become familiar with their charges and are able to rectify problems more easily.

The various horsepower figures quoted by towage companies are often confusing. The output of modern diesel engines is usually expressed in brake horsepower (bhp) or, increasingly, in kilowatts (kW); where possible bhp figures are used in this book. Brake horsepower is a figure derived from tests on the engine under load and in carefully controlled conditions. Indicated horsepower (ihp) is sometimes quoted by operators in publicity material, and was the normal means of rating engines in the days of steam. This is a calculated figure that gives a rating approximately 13 per cent higher than brake horsepower.

A feature of diesel engine design that is receiving serious consideration by engine manufacturers is the subject of smoke emission and other exhaust gas pollutants such as nitrogen oxides. In certain parts of the world, including some North American ports, port authorities are laying down regulations governing acceptable emissions from vessels working in their areas. Unfortunately the quest for more power and greater efficiency from marine engines has caused an increase in some of the more unacceptable pollutants. Further research is now well advanced to improve combustion technology in diesel engines in order to maintain high engine efficiency and at the same time meet increasingly stringent pollution-control regulations.

The fuel consumed by the modern diesel engine varies in grade but is generally of the light or gas oil type. In large sea-going tugs and oil rig supply vessels much attention has been given to improving economy. Some vessels of this type have been equipped to use cheaper, very much heavier fuel oil that would normally only be used in larger ships and steam boilers. The equipment installed to enable this fuel to be used normally comprises special heaters and a filtration plant to lower the viscosity of the oil, so that it can be burned by the diesel engine in the usual manner.

Engine installations and gearboxes
In order that the modern high-speed diesel engine can be used effectively it is necessary to provide a means of transmitting the power to the propeller or propulsion unit at a suitable rotational speed. In the case of the conventional screw propeller this is usually achieved by using a gearbox or some alternative means of power transmission such as diesel-electric or a hydraulic drive system. Azimuthing or Voith Schneider propulsion units are inherently "self-contained" and any speed reduction required is generally carried out by gear trains within the units.

The engine (or engines) used to power most conventional screw propeller systems is mounted with the drive coupling located at the after end. The gearbox is located immediately behind the engine and is designed to transmit power from the engine to the propeller at a speed calculated to give the most efficient results. Generally the gearbox has a fixed reduction ratio of somewhere between 3:1 and 7:1, thus lowering the output speed to the propeller by the same proportion. The gearbox may incorporate a reverse gear

In common with many modern propulsion systems the Voith Schneider propulsion unit has integral gearing to match engine speed and propeller efficiency. The unit shown is one of a pair in the tractor tug Redbridge. *The main engine drive shaft and the reduction gearing is in the bottom of the picture.* (Author)

and automatically operated clutch. A reverse gear may be unnecessary when controllable pitch propellers are used, as will be explained later. In most installations the gearbox and clutch controls are operated hydraulically and interconnected to the engine speed controls. A brake may be incorporated in the gearbox or on the propeller shaft to control the movement of the propeller automatically when the vessel is manoeuvring. A high degree of automation is normal in the transmission system in order to protect the engine and gearbox from damage and to simplify the controls in the wheelhouse.

In a relatively simple installation a single engine drives one propeller through a gearbox and via a rigid steel shaft. It is not uncommon, however, particularly in deep-sea tugs and oil rig supply vessels, to couple two engines to one propeller shaft. This is done by using a twin input, single output gearbox. The small size of modern diesel engines makes this a practical proposition and a four-engine installation driving twin propellers can provide an economical power plant in a sea-going vessel. The advantages of such an arrangement are that an engine can be shut down for repair or maintenance while the tug is under way on a long voyage, and when necessary the vessel can proceed more economically on only two engines, while running light without a tow.

The use of diesel-electric propulsion systems was more popular in the early days of the diesel engine, when it was quite difficult to attain good control and power at slow speeds. A diesel-electric system is one where the main engine is coupled directly to a generator, producing current to power an electric motor, which in turn drives the propeller shaft, giving precise control in a relatively simple manner via electrical switch-gear. A number of diesel engines may be used to generate power for one or more propulsion motors. Such systems are, however, very costly to manufacture and no longer compete with the modern high-speed diesel engine and gearbox installation in most towage applications. However, many diesel-electric tugs remain in operation around the world, with the majority in American ports.

Diesel-hydraulic systems operate on a similar principle. The diesel engine drives a hydraulic pump and a hydraulic motor provides power at the propeller shaft. The connection between the two can be by pipes or hoses, giving greater choice in the location of engines, etc. These systems are expensive to manufacture and are generally unsuited to high-powered installations. Diesel-hydraulic transmission systems are generally restricted to very small tugs, and also to use in bow thrust units in larger vessels.

The main engines of stern-drive and tractor tugs are located in a fore-and-aft configuration in much the same way as in a conventional screw vessel, but the means of connecting them to the propulsion units varies considerably. A brief description of the drive arrangement is included in the relevant sections that follow.

Engine controls
Engine controls have developed enormously in recent years. The days when the various engine controls were manipulated by an engineer in the engine room and communication took place via the telegraph are all but gone in the present-day tug fleet. Modern remote control systems give the tug master direct and precise control of engine speed and, where necessary, direction of rotation of the propeller shaft, via the gearbox controls. Where a controllable-pitch propeller is fitted, the pitch controls will also be operated directly from the wheelhouse, often in conjunction with the speed of the engine. The link between the engine, gearbox, and possibly the propeller pitch mechanism may be a simple mechanical linkage or a more sophisticated hydraulic, pneumatic or electronic system. In most modern tugs the engineer is provided with a control station, often in a sound-proofed cubicle, from which he can operate and monitor all of the major items of machinery. Once the tug is ready to get under way the captain is given full control of the main engine and steering systems. In some small or highly automated vessels main engine starting may also be controlled from the wheelhouse along with some of the auxiliary machinery. Even in very large vessels, highly automated engine rooms may be left unattended for long periods. Alarm systems are installed to warn of potentially serious or dangerous faults developing in propulsion or auxiliary machinery in what may be declared as Unmanned Machinery Spaces (UMS). Where this is the case alarm panels are provided in the wheelhouse and the engineer's cabin during the periods when the engine room or control room are

The engine control room of the oceangoing tug Fotiy Krylov *is the nerve centre where the performance of all four main engines, twin propellers and auxiliary machinery is monitored. Duplicate controls and computer monitoring equipment is shown on the main console and the electrical switchboards in the background.* (Author)

unmanned. An increasingly popular feature of the modern tug's engine room is a comprehensive machinery monitoring system. These computer-based systems may be used to monitor, record and display a wide range of functions. The most common functions covered are engine temperatures and pressures, cooling and fuel system performance and the liquid levels in fuel, water, ballast and other storage tanks throughout the vessel. Critical functions can be programmed with pre-set parameters to activate alarms should a malfunction occur. In many systems the information is displayed on a computer screen in the engine room control cubicle, and some or all of the data relayed to a similar, duplicate display in the wheelhouse. The data recorded in this way is available for analysis by the owner's engineering staff and is often capable of being transmitted ashore via the vessel's communications equipment.

Conventional screw propeller systems

The traditional screw propeller remains the principal means of propulsion for the great majority of tugs in one form or another. In modern tugs the conventional screw propeller is invariably used in conjunction with a nozzle or increasingly embodied in a sophisticated steerable propulsion unit. The most

49

common application remains that which employs one or more propellers located in the traditional position, under the vessel's stern, and used with or without some form of nozzle or thrust-augmenting device. As previously mentioned in Chapter 1, this arrangement without a nozzle is often referred to as an "open" propeller. These are usually found in older vessels, still continuing to give good service, or those that for operational reasons remain most suitable for local conditions in which they work.

Propeller design in any ship is a compromise, but in the tug there are a number of conflicting demands that make the designer's choice more difficult. For example, in a ship-handling tug there is a need to produce good towing characteristics at very slow speeds; at the same time the vessel must have the ability to travel quickly between tasks, and indeed be able to keep up with the ships she may be escorting. The basic factors to be considered are propeller diameter, pitch and rotational speed, and power. The propeller diameter will be governed by the hull design, operating draught, and the power to be absorbed from the power plant. Pitch can be defined as the theoretical distance the propeller will travel in one complete rotation. There are inherent inefficiency factors affecting propeller design that are too complex to be addressed here in any great detail. Propeller pitch is

The Polish tug Irbis *is a single screw Combi tug regularly carrying out coastal tows in European waters. She is seen here in dry dock in the livery of her previous owners Medway Towage and bearing the name* Kemsing. *The vessel has an "open" controllable pitch propeller, driven by a MAN main engine of 1500 bhp.* (Author)

interrelated to diameter and speed of rotation and is frequently chosen as the most convenient variable when reaching a compromise between pulling power and speed. In simple terms, for towing purposes a large propeller with a fine pitch and slow rotation produces the best results. A smaller, faster-rotating propeller with a coarser pitch would be chosen where the vessel's speed was a more important feature. In order to operate efficiently the propeller must, ideally, be deeply immersed and have a free passage for water from round the hull. As we have seen previously, several of these factors have a profound influence on the design of a tug hull. Propellers may have three, four or even five blades, depending on their application, and their shape varies widely in advanced propeller designs. Propellers intended to operate in conjunction with propulsion nozzles may have broad blades with tips that follow closely the interior diameter of the nozzle with very little clearance. Alternatively, faster-rotating propellers may have a large number of blades of a streamlined "skewed" shape. In each case the intention is to improve efficiency by avoiding phenomena known as "slip" and "cavitation"; the former is often the result of a mis-match in speed, pitch or blade design, and the latter a condition that causes air bubbles to be generated in the water flow through the propeller, causing problems with noise and vibration. The choice of materials also varies, with assorted bronze alloys, stainless steel and cast iron being the most popular.

The number of propellers installed on a tug depends very much on the type of vessel and its draught. Two propellers are frequently used where one cannot efficiently absorb the necessary power without adversely affecting the hull design and draught. A twin-screw arrangement, where each propeller is normally controlled separately, may also be chosen to enhance manoeuvrability. Three or four propellers are often used where the vessel is designed for operation in very shallow waters. Powerful pusher tugs and some multi-purpose vessels employ multiple-screw propulsion systems in order to utilise efficiently high-power main engines and keep the vessel's draught to a minimum. In order to reach an optimum arrangement for shallow-draught vessels the propellers are often located in tunnels formed in the underside of the hull.

Controllable-pitch propellers
The controllable-pitch propeller has proved to be an effective means of overcoming much of the need for compromise in propeller design. With this type of propeller the pitch of the blades can be controlled to suit the work in hand while the vessel is under way. This has the following advantages:

a) Propeller pitch can be changed automatically by a system that matches pitch to engine revolutions, giving the most efficient setting for the power available.

b) The propeller can be used to provide astern power without the need for a clutch or reverse gear in the gearbox.

c) Very fine adjustments in pitch are possible, giving precise control of thrust both forward and astern, which is particularly important when taking up the slack in a towline.

The pitch actuating mechanism is generally hydraulically operated and controlled directly from the wheelhouse; the pitch and engine speed controls are frequently combined and operated by a single lever. A disadvantage of the controllable pitch propeller is its relatively high capital cost. In some working conditions it can also be vulnerable to damage, and consequently expensive to repair. Controllable pitch propellers are frequently used in deep-sea tugs with wide operating parameters, and powerful harbour tugs equipped with Kort nozzles.

Rudders
The choice of rudder or rudders is an important feature of any tug employing conventional screw propellers. With traditional "open" screw systems a single conventional rudder located aft of each propeller is still most common. With manoeuvrability high on the tug designer's list of priorities, a great deal of development has gone into producing rudders of suitable size, area, shape and cross-section. The pivot point of the rudder and its cross-sectional shape are chosen to provide the best possible steering characteristics when the vessel is moving forward or going astern. The ability of a tug to perform well in this situation is crucial, particularly in harbour tugs. Perhaps the most important aspect of a tug's steering system is its ability to act quickly and positively. To achieve this the actuating mechanism is faster and more powerful than in many other craft, and gives greater angular movement.

Rudders are usually supported at the bottom by a pintle (hinge pin) to give added strength. Those without a lower pintle are known as the "spade" type and may be more vulnerable to damage in shallow water. In many tug designs more than one rudder is fitted. Twin rudders are sometimes used to give a single-screw tug improved steering, and are the norm in twin-screw vessels. The use of propulsion nozzles also influences rudder design, as will be seen later. In North America additional rudders, known as "flanking rudders", are sometimes fitted ahead of the propeller(s) to improve handling. Flanking rudders are common in large pusher tugs – a typical triple-screw European vessel may well have nine rudders, one aft and two forward of each propeller. There are a number of patented rudder designs utilised in tugs; some have unique cross-sectional shapes and others additional movable blades at the trailing edge to progressively change their cross-section as helm is applied. All are intended to improve the tug's turning circle and handling characteristics.

Propulsion nozzles
The propulsion nozzle was first invented in Germany in 1932 by Herr Kort and was intended originally as a device to reduce the effects of propeller wash from tugs that were causing erosion damage to the banks of German canals. It was soon apparent that the fixed tubular shroud fitted around the propeller not only had the desired effect but also considerably improved the tug's performance. Known as the "Kort nozzle", the device was soon adopted by towage concerns elsewhere in Europe and Britain. The device has been developed considerably since its inception and is now capable of producing significant improvements in performance, and the principle has been adopted,

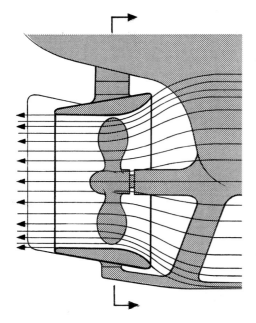

A diagram showing the flow of water through a typical Kort nozzle of the steerable type. Additional thrust generated by the action of the nozzle is shown by the arrows adjacent to the top and bottom pivot points. In a fixed nozzle thrust is transmitted to the hull through the supporting structure.

Many very small vessels are fitted with fixed propulsion nozzles. The little tug/workboat Victoria, *owned by Oprey Brothers in Belfast, has an installation typical of many. The single screw vessel has a 320 bhp main engine and a bollard pull of 4.6 tons.*

(Alan Geddes)

with various modifications, by many tug designers. To quantify the benefits of a nozzle exactly is not simple since each tug design has differing characteristics, but generally an improvement in bollard pull of between 30 and 40 per cent would be expected, when compared with an open propeller. The nozzle is basically a tube within which the propeller rotates. In cross-section the tube is tapered with an aerofoil shape on the interior. The effect of the nozzle is to cause a differential pressure between the outside and front inside surfaces, inducing additional forward thrust from the nozzle. This additional thrust is transmitted through the nozzle mountings to the vessel's hull.

Two forms of nozzle are commonly in use with conventional screw propeller systems: the fixed nozzle, which is part of the hull structure, and the steerable nozzle. The latter incorporates a rudder and is mounted on pintles in much the same way as a conventional rudder. When a steerable nozzle is used, the propeller shaft and its stern tube are extended to give the nozzle sufficient space to turn about the propeller without fouling the hull. The use of a steerable nozzle requires a particularly powerful steering mechanism to cope with the weight of the nozzle structure and the forces involved. Such an arrangement is most common in single-screw ship-handling and coastal tugs and is sometimes utilised in twin- or multiple-screw propulsion systems.

Twin Kort nozzles are fitted to the Raslanuf VII, *a tug of 2350 bhp are typical of many used on ship-handling vessels. Note the twin rudders, small central skeg and protective anodes around the nozzle casings.* (Author)

The fixed nozzle is one that encloses the propeller in the same way, but is attached firmly to the hull. This arrangement allows the use of modern rudder systems that require less powerful and less robust steering gear and is easier to incorporate in a shallow-draught vessel. Fixed-nozzle systems are frequently used in modern twin-screw tugs and are almost certain to be the choice for very large deep-sea tugs and oil rig supply vessels. Single or multiple conventional rudders may be used, or special rudders designed to increase the vessel's turning circle.

As with all modern propulsion systems, development of the Kort and similar nozzle systems continues and various enhancements are available to suit particular vessels and conditions. One such development that emerged some years ago but which has not grown greatly in popularity is the "Towmaster" system. Used on a variety of tug types, from harbour tugs to ocean-going vessels, the system is based on a fixed nozzle type not unlike the Kort design. The main difference is in the rudder system used. Rudders, described as "shutter rudders", are positioned ahead and astern of the nozzle; often three rudders are located astern and two (flanking rudders) ahead. The shutter rudders closely control the flow of water through the propeller and nozzle, improving both pulling performance and manoeuvrability. The Towmaster system has been used with some success in several new vessels and when installed in existing tugs to improve performance.

A "Towmaster" nozzle and rudder system (left) is fitted to the fire fighting tug Ted Noffs *of the Australian Maritime Services Board. Each set of specially shaped triple rudders is capable of being controlled independently to enhance manoeuvrability. The vessel was built in 1986 and has two controllable pitch propellers, driven by main engines producing a total of 1400 bhp and a bollard pull of 21 tonnes.* (Burness, Corlett & Partners)

Propellers used in conjunction with propulsion nozzles of the Kort type can be of the fixed or controllable type, with the latter becoming increasingly popular; the blade profile of these propellers is specially chosen for operation inside a nozzle. A particular problem encountered in many nozzle systems is that of electrolytic erosion of propeller blades, nozzle, and hull plating caused by the use of dissimilar metals – eg a bronze propeller rotating in close proximity to a steel nozzle. In order to combat this problem zinc blocks known as anodes, which work on a sacrificial principle, are fitted to the exterior of the nozzle(s) and surrounding hull structure. Stainless steel may also be used for the internal surface of the nozzle to resist erosion and wear caused by sand and other particles in the water flowing through the nozzle.

Propulsion nozzles are also used in conjunction with many propulsion units of the azimuthing type covered later in this chapter. The nozzle structure forms an integral part of the steerable propeller unit, but the principles involved are identical to those described previously.

Controls in conventional tugs
To complete this section on conventional tug propulsion systems mention must be made of the engine and steering controls located in the wheelhouse. The actual controls fitted vary considerably with the type of tug and the owner's specific preferences. For example, a single-screw ship-handling tug, with a controllable-pitch propeller, may have a single lever to control engine speed and, within limits, propeller pitch. The combination of pitch and engine speed can often be adjusted in relation to each other by push-button switches or some similar means. To manoeuvre ahead or astern the pitch lever is used, moved progressively forward to move the tug ahead, and backwards to go astern. The same fine degree of control is possible in either direction.

A similar arrangement is used where a fixed-pitch propeller and gearbox are used to control forward and astern movement. The engine speed and gearbox

One of two sets of propulsion controls on the twin screw 1014 bhp tug Zwerver I. *Engine speed and forward and astern gears are controlled by the two levers on the left. The centre lever in the foreground steers the vessel and the lever on the right controls the bow thruster. Controls on the top right of the panel operate the towing winch.*   *(Author)*

forward and reverse gears are commonly controlled by a single lever, with a central neutral position. Again, the lever is moved forward to move ahead and backwards to go astern. In twin-screw tugs the two controls are normally mounted side by side and enable the propellers to be controlled independently and precisely.

A similar vessel would be steered either by a wheel, a small lever, or even a pair of push-buttons; in conventional tugs of any size steering wheels are frequently fitted for emergency use only. Small steering levers are most common and a number may be installed, conveniently located with engine and other controls at strategic positions in the wheelhouse, and sometimes at vantage points outside.

For the same reason steering (and sometimes engine) controls are fitted to a small portable hand unit, connected by an electric cable to the control systems, to enable the captain to position himself in full view of the work in hand.

Azimuthing propulsion units

Azimuthing propulsion unit is an unwieldy but universal title given to a great many propulsion units of a similar type and produced by a number of manufacturers; the terms "rudder propeller" and "Z drive unit" are also used. The trade names Aquamaster, Duckpeller, Z-Peller, Schottel and Compass all apply to units of a similar type that are widely used the towage industry.

An azimuthing propulsion unit is basically a conventional screw propeller that is driven through a system of gears in such a way that the entire propeller and its shaft can be rotated about a vertical axis – in much the same way as an outboard motor. Most units can be turned through a full 360 degrees, enabling thrust from the propeller to be used to propel and steer the vessel in any desired direction. The majority of units incorporate a nozzle of the Kort type to improve thrust and have fixed-pitch propellers. The unit's inherent gear train enables the propeller speed to be matched to the pitch of the propeller and the performance required with relative ease. In high-powered tugs the use of fixed-pitch propellers can make precise control difficult at very slow speeds, for example when taking up the slack in a towline. To improve this feature of their performance either a controllable-pitch propeller is used, or more commonly a device is fitted in the drive system to enable the propellers to turn very slowly indeed. This takes the form of a fluid drive or a slipping clutch arrangement, which is controlled automatically with the speed of the engine.

The propulsion unit is self-contained. An upper gearbox casing bolts into the hull of the tug and contains not only gears to drive the propeller but also the steering mechanism and a lubrication system. A drive shaft connects the unit to the engine and the only other services required are electrical or hydraulic to control the steering gear.

Azimuthing propulsion units are used in tugs for main propulsion or as bow thrusters. As previously described in Chapter 1, twin units may be installed beneath the stern of the vessel in the stern-drive configuration, or alternatively in the forward part of the hull in the tractor mode. When employed as a bow thruster the unit is generally fitted with a retracting mechanism to enable it to be housed within the hull when not in use.

In a stern-drive tug twin azimuthing propulsion units are invariably employed and located beneath the vessel's stern. The position of the units, with the gearboxes located high in the hull, requires complex shafting

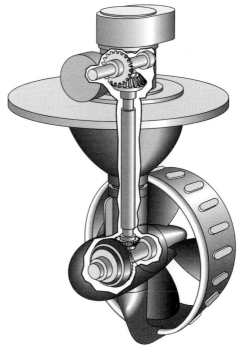

The diagram depicts the "Z" drive configuration of a typical azimuthing propulsion unit, cut away to show the drive shafts and gears. The steering gear, which turns the entire centre portion and propeller through 360 degrees, is omitted for clarity.

to transmit power from the engines, which for the purposes of weight distribution and stability must remain low in the structure. The drive shafts are fitted with large flexible joints in order to accommodate the differing heights of engine and propulsion unit, and great care is taken with the design and installation of the shafts in order to avoid problems with excessive noise and vibration.

One of the main advantages of the stern-drive configuration is that a very high bollard pull can be attained, coupled with impressive handling characteristics, yet without greatly increasing the draught of the vessel. Properly handled, the stern-drive tug can move ahead, astern or sideways and turn within its own length. To achieve these manoeuvres the units are turned, in unison or individually, to a whole range of positions designed to produce the correct thrust for the evolution required. The accompanying diagram shows the relative positions of the units for basic manoeuvres.

One of the most important features of a stern-drive tug of this type is that its bollard pull when towing astern is almost equal to that produced going ahead. This is of great significance in a ship-handling and escort tug, and a feature that is impossible to reproduce in a conventional screw vessel.

This impressive view shows the twin Schottel azimuthing propulsion units in the stern of the type ASD 3110 tug Citta Della Spezia *built by Damen Shipyard for Rimorchiatori Riuniti Spezzini of Naples. The clean lines of the hull beneath the stern and controllable pitch propellers are clearly visible.* (Damen Shipyard)

Controls in stern-drive tugs with azimuthing units
Control of the azimuthing units in this type of vessel is quite a complex process, inspiring many ingenious control systems devised to simplify matters for the tug captain. An electro-hydraulic system is generally used to control the steering movements of each unit and the rotational speed of the propeller. In the wheelhouse, controls vary from a complicated array of individual engine and steering controls for each unit to computer-controlled systems that enable a

The diagram illustrates the relative positions of the propulsion units in a stern drive tug to accomplish the basic manoeuvres indicated by the arrows. The same basic techniques apply to a tractor tug fitted with azimuthing units.

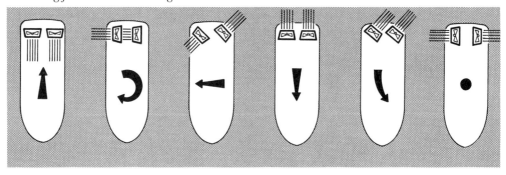

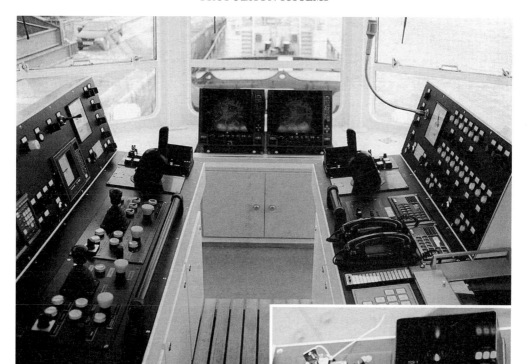

single lever to be used to manoeuvre the vessel. Some operators and crews prefer separate individual controls, which appear daunting to the outsider and usually take the form of a single handle, incorporating a speed control, used to "steer" each unit individually. In the controls of most azimuthing-unit tugs there is no neutral or reverse position for propeller rotation. When the vessel is at rest the propellers continue to rotate but are turned outboard as shown in the diagram. To move forward the units are progressively turned to direct thrust towards the stern. Moving astern is accomplished by turning the units through 180 degrees, directing the thrust forward. Each unit can be rotated using a separate lever, and indicators show the position of each unit in relation to the hull. More complicated manoeuvres are carried

In the stern drive tug Portgarth *the master stands between the two control consoles, facing in the direction the tug is to travel, with the individual combined steering and propeller controls – one in each hand. Each control (inset) allows the engine speed to be adjusted and the unit to be rotated through 360 degrees. An indicator to show the direction of thrust is located adjacent to the lever.* (Author)

out by moving the units as shown in the diagram, and applying differing amounts of power. In some systems a small steering wheel is used to steer a course in the normal way with the units turning in unison, either ahead or astern.

When a single-lever control system is installed, an electronic micro-processor controls all of the required functions – the lever is simply moved in the direction the tug is required to travel. In some systems the engine speed control is separate, in others it is incorporated in the lever mechanism. Whatever the control system, the speed and precision with which the units can be rotated through the full 360-degree steering arc is most important.

Azimuthing propulsion systems in tractor tugs
The azimuthing propulsion units used in tractor tugs are of the same basic design as those previously described in stern-drive vessels. Their location beneath the forward hull simplifies to some degree the installation of units and engines and reduces the need for very long and complex drive shafting. Other factors relating to the design and comparison of tractors with azimuthing and Voith Schneider propulsion units was covered in Chapter 1.

Controls in tractor tugs with azimuthing units
Similar principles apply to the control of the azimuthing unit tractor as those previously described for the stern-drive type of vessel. The propulsion units are rotated to much the same positions, in relation to each other and the hull, to achieve similar manoeuvres. Handling characteristics will be different due to the presence of the large skeg, but the azimuthing unit position diagram remains valid for the tractor configuration. Controls in the wheelhouse also follow much the same basic pattern, with various manufacturers using the same systems regardless of whether the vessel is a tractor or stern-drive tug.

One of the many alternative control systems for azimuthing propulsion units is the Schottel Masterpilot. A single central control is used to manoeuvre the vessel in any direction. The small lever above the control wheel governs propeller speed. If required the Masterpilot can be disengaged and the units controlled by the individual controllers located at either side.

(Schottel)

Voith Schneider propulsion units
The present-day Voith Schneider propulsion unit is based on the unique cycloidal propeller invented by Ernst Schneider and J. M. Voith in 1928. The propeller is unlike any conventional screw propeller or paddle mechanism. In current practice, Voith Schneider propulsion units are almost exclusively fitted in tugs of the tractor type, which originally evolved hand in hand with the Voith Schneider system. As mentioned in Chapter 1, most of the early development

took place in Germany, but the Voith tractor tug soon became popular in other European countries. Acceptance of this type of propulsion has taken some time to spread elsewhere, but examples are now in use in ports throughout the world.

With the exception of very small tugs, and a number of earlier vessels, most modern tractors are fitted with two propulsion units, side by side. Each propulsion unit has a series of blades, pointing downwards, attached to a hub that rotates about a vertical axis. Each blade has a hydrofoil cross-section, and at a predetermined position in the blades' circular path, a change of pitch occurs producing propulsive thrust. The action is not unlike the sculling action of an oar, but uses circular rather than the more complex oscillating motion. The circular path around which the blades travel is known as a cycloid – hence the name cycloidal propeller. The point in the blades' path at which the change of pitch takes place is controlled by a mechanical linkage, comprising levers and cranks known as the

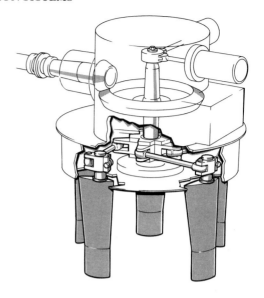

This very much simplified diagram of a Voith Schneider propulsion unit shows the principle components of the cycloidal propeller and its control mechanism. The cut-away section depicts the kinematic linkage which controls the pitch of each blade as the assembly rotates. In the centre is the control rod, connected at the top to its two servo actuators. The input shaft enters from the left and, through bevel gearing, drives the entire rotor assembly.

"kinematics", located inside the hub (or rotor) of the propeller. At the centre of the linkage is a control rod that determines the position where the change in blade pitch occurs and the magnitude of that change. In this way thrust can be vectored in any chosen direction in relation to the hull and its force controlled with great precision. The accompanying diagram shows a simplified blade arrangement and the way that thrust is generated and directed.

In practice, the number of blades used and the diameter of the blade path, or orbit, is chosen to match the power available and the size of vessel. The thrust available when going ahead or astern is almost identical and changes very little throughout the 360-degree steering circle. The Voith system affords a degree of control superior to most others, but in terms of propeller efficiency the cycloidal unit compares less favourably with those utilising the screw propeller.

Each propulsion unit is self-contained. The main casing embodies a mounting flange to secure the unit to the hull structure, and encloses the gear train to drive the hub of the propeller and the necessary lubrication system. Located in the top of the casing is the hydraulic servo mechanism used to

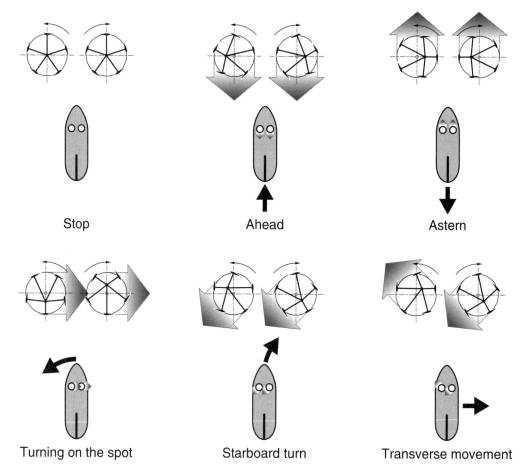

Stop   Ahead   Astern

Turning on the spot   Starboard turn   Transverse movement

The diagram illustrates the propulsion units of a twin unit Voith tractor tug, showing where changes of pitch occur in the blade orbit and the direction of the resulting thrust in relation to the hull. Control positions have been chosen to illustrate the direction of thrust required to perform the basic manoeuvres indicated.

operate the control rod. The wheelhouse controls are connected to this servo mechanism, usually by means of mechanical linkage.

The installation of the units and main engines is similar to that of the azimuthing tractor, with the engines low in the hull and a simple shaft drive to the units. The hull design also incorporates a large skeg at the stern and a protection plate fitted below the propellers as described in Chapter 1; this is often referred to as the "nozzle plate". It was discovered early in the development of the Voith tractor that the plate could be given a certain hydrodynamic cross-sectional shape and used to improve the flow of water and consequently thrust. The effect is similar to that of the nozzle surrounding a conventional screw propeller. In common with other tractor tug designs, the Voith Schneider-propelled vessel tends to have a relatively deep draught.

The operating characteristics of the propulsion units allow the main engines of a Voith tractor tug to run at a constant speed. Once the engines are started and the propellers rotating, all further control can be carried out using the unit's pitch controls. A useful by-product of having a constant engine speed is that auxiliary machinery can be driven directly from either engine. In fire-fighting tugs this is particularly advantageous, enabling high-capacity fire pumps to be driven from the main engines, yet leaving enough power available to manoeuvre the tug.

Controls in tractor tugs with Voith Schneider units
The controls of a Voith Schneider trac-tor tug are extremely simple and always take the same form. In the wheelhouse the captain is provided with a steering wheel and pitch levers; the number of the latter depends on whether the vessel has one or two propulsion units, one pitch lever being used to control

The German tractor tug Blumental, *seen prior to launch, is typical of many similar vessels in use in Europe. Here Voith Schneider propulsion units are visible above the protection plate and its supporting struts.* (Voith Schneider)

each unit. These controls are located on what is known as a control stand and may be duplicated where necessary. One central control stand is fitted in the most modern ship-handling tractors. Alternatively, one stand is located at the front and one at the rear of the wheelhouse to give the tug captain a choice of operating position.

In very simple terms, the steering wheel controls transverse thrust and the pitch levers longitudinal thrust. The pitch levers have a central neutral position and as they are moved forward or backwards pitch is progressively increased in the ahead or astern direction respectively. Movement of the steering wheel vectors thrust to either side as required to steer the vessel. Small movements of the wheel produce changes in heading similar to any other steering systems, but as more wheel is applied increasing sideways thrust is produced. With the wheel turned to its full extent in either direction, only sideways thrust is produced by the propulsion units.

The two pitch levers fitted in twin-unit tractors are generally located side by side and enable the longitudinal pitch component produced by each unit to be controlled separately. In modern control stands the levers may be manipulated independently or in unison without restriction. This gives extremely precise control when manoeuvring and enables the tug to turn in little more than its own length. Earlier versions of the control stand incorporated a simple latch to allow the levers to be locked together and moved as one when required.

A device is also fitted to most control stands to limit the maximum movement of the pitch levers under certain conditions. This takes to form of a small additional lever or simple limiting flaps on the lever quadrant. The purpose of this device is to prevent maximum pitch being selected under circumstances

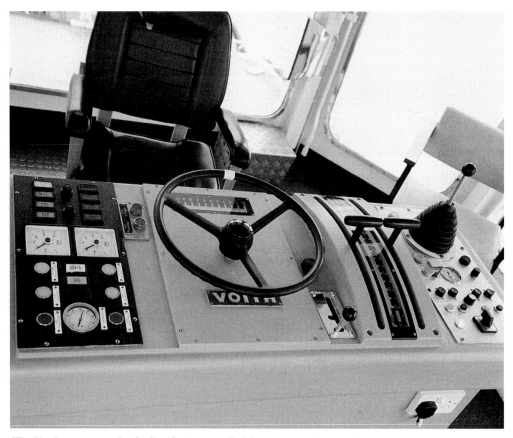

The Voith tractor tug Lady Sarah *is controlled from a central console in the wheelhouse. The levers on the right of the wheel control the pitch of the propeller blades. A small lever, in the foreground, has three positions and limits the maximum pitch that can be applied in different modes of operation. Two rows of buttons on the left control engine speed. The panel on the extreme right contains the towing winch controls.* (Author)

that might overload the main engine(s). For example, in the modern fire-fighting tractor a lever marked "Free Running", "Towing" and "Fire Fighting" allows units to be used at maximum pitch when the vessel is running light between operations; subject to some restriction when towing; and subject to further restriction during fire-fighting operations to enable power from the main engines to be used to drive the fire pumps but with sufficient in hand to manoeuvre the vessel.

As mentioned previously, the propulsion units are designed to operate at a constant engine speed. The most common arrangement is to provide the tug master with a number of pre-set speed ranges that can be selected by means of push buttons, located on or adjacent to the control stand. Typically four buttons are provided for each engine and annotated "MIN", "75%", "85%" and "MAX". The annotations are self-explanatory and indicate the engine speed range to be selected, to suit the conditions under which the vessel is operating.

Bow thrusters

The term "bow thruster" is a familiar one in shipping circles, and various forms of bow thruster are used in ships of all sizes as a means of improving their handling characteristics in port. In fact, the installation of such units in large numbers of medium-sized ships has contributed greatly to a reduction in demand for ship-handling tugs. Bow thrusters are used in tugs for two reasons. The simple transverse thruster has become increasingly popular in tugs of all types, with the exception of tractors, to improve handling and station-keeping in difficult conditions. More sophisticated, azimuthing propulsion units may be fitted in the bows of ship-handling tugs to enhance their manoeuvrability and versatility.

Transverse thrusters

The most common form of transverse thruster found in a tug comprises a simple tube passing through the bow of the vessel. A conventional screw propeller installed in the tube provides thrust at 90 degrees to the vessel's centreline. The direction of thrust, to port or starboard, is controlled

A transverse bow thruster is fitted in the naval, stern drive, tug Impulse *as indicated by the tubular duct below the waterline and the "star" shaped warning sign on the hull. Her bow fendering is carried right to the bottom of the stem to avoid causing damage when working with submarines.*

(Ray Johnson)

by changing either the rotational direction of the propeller or the pitch of the blades. Power to drive the propeller is produced either by an electric motor, a hydraulic motor, or a diesel engine. In deep-sea tugs the bow thruster may be quite a powerful unit driven by a power plant of 600 bhp or more. Very large vessels may have one or two transverse thrusters fitted in the bow and a further unit located aft, usually just forward of the propellers. Electric motors or hydraulic drives generally derive their power from auxiliary machinery in the engine room. A diesel engine coupled directly to the thruster is also used, but requires considerably more space in the normally cramped forecastle of the tug.

Transverse thrusters are generally controlled directly from the bridge by a simple lever, mounted athwartships, adjacent to the normal steering and propulsion controls. The lever is moved to port or starboard in the direction in which the bow of the vessel is required to move. Multiple thrusters, fitted in the bow and stern of large offshore vessels, may be controlled separately or as part of an integrated manoeuvring system.

The azimuthing thruster

The azimuthing thruster used in this application is identical in basic design to those used as main propulsion units. Thrusters of this type are most frequently installed in single-screw tugs to fit them for a particular task and possibly extend their useful life. As described in Chapter 1, the term "combi-tug" is often used to describe a vessel equipped in this way. The thruster unit is installed in the forward part of the hull, close to the bow. Most units are retractable and housed within the hull when not in use, which has the added advantage of enabling the vessel to return to her original draught when necessary, possibly to prevent damage in shallow water.

The thruster may be driven by a separate diesel engine, or an electric or hydraulic motor; a power plant of between 400 and 650 bhp is common. In a harbour tug space is at a premium in the forward part of the vessel, and crew accommodation is often sacrificed to make room for the unit, its retracting mechanism and power plant. Where a separate diesel engine is used to drive the unit, a mechanism is incorporated in the power transmission system to disconnect the thruster from the engine as it retracts.

Irbis, *mentioned earlier, is a Combi tug with retractable azimuthing thruster fitted in the bow. The unit is shown lowered into its working position.* (Author)

The thruster is normally controlled from the wheelhouse using a single lever enabling the unit to be "steered" through 360 degrees and propeller revolutions to be adjusted. In most cases the lever is very similar to those used in stern-drive vessels to control individual propulsion units.

Integrated control systems

Many large tugs and offshore support vessels make extensive use of an integrated control system, to enable the vessel to be manoeuvred simply by means of a single lever. The "single lever" control system in this context enables the vessel's rudders, propellers, bow and stern thrusters to be operated in unison under the control of a micro-processor. This obviates the need for the tug master to co-ordinate the use of separate controls for each of those functions. Using a lever often referred to as a "joystick", the vessel can be moved precisely forward, astern, to port or starboard and bodily sideways by simply moving the lever in the desired direction of travel. Most systems also make use of inputs from the gyro compass or automatic pilot to control the vessel's heading, an important advantage to the master of a relatively large vessel manoeuvring in offshore locations. In order to be fully effective the computer control system is programmed to suit the individual vessel, taking into account the response and power output of each element of the propulsion system and the handling characteristics of the ship.

A control console in the wheelhouse of a modern oil rig supply vessel houses controls for the main engine, propeller and bow thruster (centre rear). In the right lower panel is the "Joystick" of an integrated control system and the electronic controls and indicators used to control the vessel's heading. *(Ulstein)*

CHAPTER 3

Towing gear and deck equipment

The towing gear on board any tug provides an indispensable link between the vessel herself and the ship or other floating object to be towed. A modern tug, whatever its role, must still rely on the modern equivalent of a simple towrope to make that vital connection. A phenomenally high bollard pull and impressive manoeuvrability can only be used to good effect if applied to the tow in a safe and efficient manner. The demands made on towing gear by the current generation of tugs is greater than ever before; as bollard pulls have progressively increased, considerable effort has been applied to the design of towropes themselves and the equipment required to handle them safely. Commercial pressures demand that the work must be done quickly, with the smallest acceptable crew, and this has placed greater emphasis on new lightweight towing gear and advanced deck equipment. This is particularly true in the case of powerful escort tugs and larger vessels designed to work offshore.

In spite of its long history the towage industry has not successfully dispensed with the towrope as the primary means of connecting tug and tow. The types of ropes used and the gear to handle them are continually changing, but many old-established principles remain valid. Alternative methods of establishing a towing connection appear from time to time but none have succeeded in replacing the humble towline to any great extent. Push-towing may be considered the exception, but this specialised application is dealt with in a later chapter dedicated to pusher tugs.

The use of huge suction pads, connected to the tug by hydraulically controlled arms and capable of firmly attaching themselves to a ship's side, were introduced in Japan some years ago as a possible alternative towing connection for ship-handling. However, the towage industry worldwide has showed no great interest in this approach, but has tended to consider more seriously new methods of putting conventional towlines aboard ships, using mechanical line-handling devices.

The towrope
The terms "towrope" or "towline" are often applied to both fibre and steel wire ropes used for towing. The modern fibre towrope is a very different piece of equipment from that used in tugs 50 years ago. Before the introduction of synthetic textiles in rope production, the towing industry relied on natural

The towline remains the vital link between tug and tow in the majority of towage operations. In this example a "multiple plaited" rope of man-made fibres is being used by a conventional screw tug, in conjunction with a quick release towing hook. (*Author*)

materials such as manila and hemp. Ropes made from these materials were heavy and very difficult to handle when wet, and once waterlogged they rapidly sank, presenting a hazard to the tug by possibly fouling her propeller. The size of rope required by a powerful tug of the day was enormous, often as large as 1 foot (300 mm) in diameter.

Modern man-made fibre ropes are manufactured using a variety of materials and sometimes complex construction methods to produce operating characteristics tailored exactly to meet the needs of the tug owner. Polypropylene, polyester, nylon, aramid and high modulus polyethylene (HMPE) synthetic fibres are among the more commonly used basic materials now used for towrope manufacture. The latter is a modern ultra-high-strength material, marketed around the world under the names Dymeema and Spectra. The construction of modern towropes varies considerably, and new approaches continue to be introduced to meet demands for greater strength, lightness in weight, buoyancy, resistance to wear and many other factors. The towline used by a powerful ship-handling tug may well be subjected to loads in excess of 100 tonnes, yet must be light and flexible enough to be manhandled aboard the tug and the vessel to be towed. Most of the modern generation of synthetic fibre towropes are buoyant and impervious to the likely forms of contamination encountered on board tugs, but they still need to be used with care. In many types of rope considerable internal friction is generated under extreme loads, particularly where they pass through fairleads, around bollards, and in knots. The heat generated inside the ropes under these circumstances can cause the strands to melt and the rope to fail.

Many modern ropes are no longer spun in the traditional manner but incorporate various methods of plaiting and multiple plaiting. In some recent products the internal strands of the rope are only slightly twisted and not plaited in any way. Known by various trade names such as "Superline", the strands are kept tightly secured by a strong woven sheath, which maintains the shape of the rope and protects the load-bearing strands from external damage. One example of this type of construction uses HMPE fibres and is intended to replicate, as far as possible, the strength and operating characteristics of a steel wire towline, but with a vast reduction in weight and much improved handling characteristics. Such ropes must be capable of operating successfully on modern towing winches and, because of their relatively high cost, must have a long working life.

Nylon was the first synthetic material to be used in the towing industry. It had many advantages over early natural fibres, but also several disadvantages. Nylon ropes stretch considerably in use and are extremely elastic, both of which features make them difficult to use in many towage applications, particularly in ship-handling. The material still has special uses, where those characteristics are advantageous; in deep-sea towing its elasticity is utilised by connecting short lengths of large-diameter nylon rope into steel towlines to act as "springs".

Steel wire towropes, or hawsers, have for very many years been used in offshore operations and in all types of long-distance towing. This type of rope is also used in many harbour tugs where a towing winch is used. As in the past, the ropes are manufactured from high-grade, cold drawn steel wire, spun in the traditional manner. The main advances in the production of the modern steel wire rope are the use of more sophisticated grades of steel and the protective treatments applied. During manufacture, and in use, the ropes are treated with advanced synthetic lubricants designed to reduce internal friction and resist damage from salt water.

Combinations of steel and fibre rope are often used in a single towline. In harbour tugs a short length of wire rope is frequently used at the outer end of the fibre towrope. This is known as the "pendant" and is used to resist the loads and chafing that occurs where the towline passes through the fairleads and around the bitts on board the tow. As previously mentioned, short lengths of fibre rope are also used in conjunction with steel towropes to provide a degree of elasticity. In recent practice, modern synthetic fibre towlines may also incorporate a pendant manufactured from a synthetic material of a different type. The pendant material will be chosen to afford more elasticity, better wear resistance, or to simply provide an easily replaceable element at the end of an expensive towline.

Chain cable is rarely used as part of the actual towline due to the difficulty in handling this material and its weight. It is, however, often used as part of the towing connection, between the towline and tow. Chafing is the main enemy to all towlines, particularly at the point at which they are secured to the tow. In long-distance towing a single length of chain cable, or a "Y"-shaped bridle, is used to make the connection aboard a tow such as a ship or large barge. The weight of chain in the bridle also acts as a spring to reduce the effects of snatching in bad weather.

Towing bollards

In many earlier tugs, particularly in Holland and the USA, the primary means of securing the towropes aboard was by using towing bollards. These take the form of large "H"-shape bollards on which the rope is secured in a particular way. The method of "turning the rope up" on the bollards varies from country to country and port to port, and is intended to give the crewman on deck the means to secure the rope quickly at the appropriate length. Where American towing methods are used, towing bollards will be fitted on the foredeck and on the towing deck aft. This method of securing the inboard end of a towrope is still used in many tugs, but with modern high-powered vessels it is impractical and unsafe. Many of the modern synthetic fibre ropes previously mentioned do not lend themselves to this method of towing without being damaged if high bollard pulls are involved. Towing

Towing bollards are used by many operators of small and relatively low powered tugs as a convenient means of securing the towline aboard the tug. Here, a small ship is being towed by a tug/workboat with the towline "turned up" on bollards in a manner which will allow it to be released quickly in an emergency. (Author)

bollards are, however, convenient in some applications and are often incorporated in the fairlead of a towing winch or the mounting of a towing hook as a secondary means of securing a rope end.

Towing hooks

A common method of securing the inboard end of a towrope is a towing hook. This method is universal in most British and European tugs, when a towing winch is not fitted. Even when the towline is normally handled by a winch, a hook is generally provided as a secondary means of securing a rope. The main advantage of the tow hook is its ease of use and the ability to release the tow instantly in an emergency.

There are many designs of quick-release tow hook, all of which are designed to enable the towline to be released easily and quickly if the tug is endangered by the risk of capsizing or any similar hazard. To release the towline, the hook is generally designed to open or swing down, letting the rope slip away. This

A typical quick-release towing hook, shown in the closed position. To release the rope in an emergency, the lanyard visible above the hook is used to trip a release mechanism – causing the circular portion of the hook to rotate and release the rope. *(Author)*

mechanism must be capable of operating even under the extreme loads imposed on the towline when the tug is towing or being dragged at full power. In early designs the release mechanism was a simple one, normally activated manually by a large hammer wielded by a member of the crew. Present-day hooks are usually released by remote control, a much safer procedure. The release mechanism may be operated via a pneumatic or hydraulic system, or by a cable, with controls duplicated in the wheelhouse and on deck.

Many tugs, particularly conventional screw vessels, have their tow hook located on a righting arm. With this type of mounting the hook is fitted on a long radial arm, which is free to pivot on the centreline of the vessel but allows the hook to swing through an arc to either side. A semi-circular track is usually fitted to guide the righting arm and hook. This arrangement is a safety feature and designed to reduce the likelihood of the tug being accidentally capsized when the towline is directly abeam of the vessel.

Towing winches
Towing winches were first introduced in tugs to handle the very long towropes used in ocean towing. Such towing gear was extremely heavy and there was a need to find a means of shortening and retrieving the towline quickly and safely. The basic purpose of the towing winch has changed very little, but most modern tugs of any size are fitted with winches to ease the workload on board and allow the tug captain to control the towline remotely from the wheelhouse. The winches currently in use are of two main types, the traditional drum type and the friction winch.

Drum winches

The drum winch is by far the most common type of winch used in the towage industry. It is basically a power-driven drum, or barrel, on which the towline is wound. This type of winch is produced in many sizes and with many variations, but the principle remains the same. In modern harbour ship-handling tugs a typical towing winch is likely to be fitted with a single drum, driven by an electric or hydraulic motor. The forward and reverse controls of the winch and a powerful brake are normally located in the wheelhouse. The winch will be sufficiently powerful to retrieve the towline and, with the brake applied, can withstand a pull well in excess of the tug's bollard pull, although a ship-handling tug may not necessarily be equipped with a winch powerful enough to shorten the towline with the vessel at full power. The winch will handle either a steel wire towrope or one made of synthetic fibres.

Many tugs of the azimuthing stern-drive type are equipped with two drum winches, one aft and one on the fore deck. In this type of vessel, used for ship-handling and escort work, the forward winch is generally the principal means of making a towing connection. A winch used in this way will often have a single drum, partitioned to enable two towlines of different characteristics to be carried and available for immediate use. The forward winch may also incorporate a windlass to handle the vessel's anchors. Devices to monitor the length of the towline in use and the load to which it is subjected are becoming increasingly common in sophisticated escort tugs.

Drum winches fitted in tugs designed for coastal and deep-sea towing will almost certainly be more powerful and may have more than one drum. Two or even three drums, side by side on a single shaft and controlled independently,

The forward towing winch shown is typical of many drum winches fitted to stern drive tugs as the principle means of making a towing connection. This example, aboard the Cramond, *has provision for two towlines and incorporates an anchor windlass.* (*Author*)

A drum winch of the waterfall type is common on anchor-handling tugs and oil rig supply vessels such as the Far Turbot. *This picture shows the two main drums, mounted one above the other. Also visible, at deck level, are two small tugger winches. Stowed adjacent to the winch opening is a "J" hook and grapple. The power operated drum in the top right is used to store pennants and spare wires.* (Author)

are common. The drums will contain either identical towlines or towlines of different dimensions, to be used for different purposes. Winches installed in large deep-sea tugs may also incorporate a device to limit and control the tension on the towline. When in use the winch will pay out or wind in automatically to compensate for abnormal shock loads, but keep the towline at approximately the required length. The winches will be located on the towing deck aft, totally or partially enclosed within the superstructure to afford some protection from the elements.

A winch known as the "waterfall" type has two or more drums mounted in tandem, with each drum a little higher than its neighbour. Winches with two or three drums are used extensively in anchor-handling tugs and oil rig supply vessels. One drum of the winch will accommodate a special wire rope and have sufficient power to handle the very large anchors used by oil drilling rigs and similar floating plant.

A limitation of the drum-type winch, particularly where very high bollard pulls are involved, is that the outer layers of rope on the drum tend to tighten excessively. This causes crushing and damage to the layers of rope near the centre of the drum.

Friction winches

The friction winch, sometimes known as a twin-drum capstan winch, is a fairly recent innovation in the towage industry. It was originally introduced in very powerful deep-sea tugs to overcome some of the deficiencies of the drum winch, and employs two grooved friction drums arranged parallel to each other (see the accompanying diagram) and driven in unison; the towline passes around both drums about five times. A third drum, simply a large reel, acts as a storage drum for the inboard end of the rope. The storage drum applies a small load to the inboard end of the rope, keeping tension on the turns around the friction drums. In this way the rope is wound in or out using the capstan principle, relying on the friction between the drum grooves and the rope.

There are a number of significant advantages to this system. Perhaps the most important is that no crushing or deformation of the rope occurs. The winch in a large sea-going tug is generally located inside the superstructure, and with the friction winch, the twin drums can be placed in the most practical position, from a towing point of view, and the storage drum located well below decks. This enables the great weight of the steel towlines to be kept low in the vessel, thus contributing to the tug's stability. A tug of this type may have many hundreds of metres of towline on board, including spare material.

A friction winch, of the type used in large oceangoing tugs, uses two grooved drums to impart motion to the towline in much the same manner as a capstan. The lower storage drum is generally located well below decks and contains the bulk of what is often a very long steel wire rope.

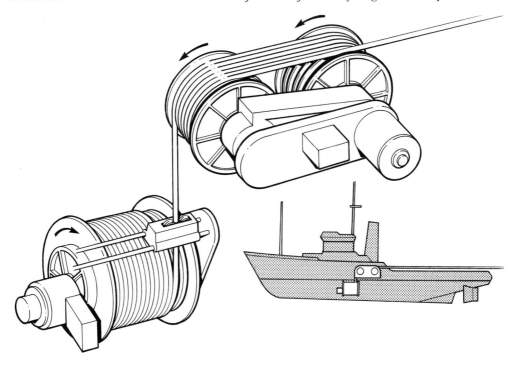

A friction drum winch is shown here aboard the Japanese built tug Lady Morag *to handle a man-made fibre towline. The turns of rope can be seen on the friction drums and leading to the storage drum on the left. The outer end of the towline passes through a heavy fairlead in the bow of the vessel.* (*Author*)

The friction winch is also used to handle synthetic fibre towropes. In Britain and elsewhere a number of ship-handling tugs have been built with winches of this type using exactly the same principle as those designed for steel wire towlines. In this application the winch is generally more compact with the storage drum incorporated in the winch structure or in a convenient location elsewhere in the vessel.

Tugger winches
The term "tugger winch" is common in the salvage and offshore oil industry and refers to small auxiliary drum winches used extensively aboard deep-sea tugs and anchor-handling vessels. Such winches are commonly fitted or either side of the main towing deck and sometimes on a higher level at the after end of the superstructure.

The main purpose of the tugger winch is to provide a means of handling the outer ends of the main towing wires on the tug's afterdeck. In many cases the towlines are too large and heavy to be manhandled or manipulated by means of a capstan. Large pieces of towing gear such as chain bridles and equipment used in anchor handling will be moved around the deck using the wires from one or more tugger winches. In some vessels a tugger winch may be used to control a gog rope used to secure the main towline – see the following section.

Gog ropes and restraining devices

"Gog rope" is a British term that refers to a rope used to control the movement of the main towline in ship-handling and deep-sea tugs. The term "gob rope" and "bridle" are also commonly used in some localities for the same item; "bridle" is also a name used to describe a "Y"-shaped towing connection used between a towline and tow.

Conventional screw ship-handling tugs, working with a ship in difficult conditions, may use the gog rope to hold the towrope down, at a position close to her stern, thus effectively moving the towing connection aft. This procedure gives the tug captain better control of his tow and prevents the towline from being taken across the tug's beam, thus subjecting her to the danger of being capsized. A deep-sea tug may secure her tow in a similar manner, also to prevent a long heavy towrope from getting over her beam, to port or starboard. A deep-sea tug or oil rig supply vessel may also use its hydraulically operated line-handling equipment to secure the towline, with similar results.

Tugs using gog ropes are fitted with a large steel eye or fairlead on deck, in a position a little forward of the rudder post(s). The gog rope passes through this eye and is looped over the towline or attached by a free-running shackle. The inner end of the rope is controlled by a small winch fitted for the purpose, a capstan, or simply by securing it to bollards.

When a gog rope is used the point at which the towline is secured aboard the tug is effectively moved to a location much further aft. The length of the gog rope is often controlled by a small winch or by a capstan. The inset shows an alternative method of securing a towline using hydraulically controlled line handling gear.

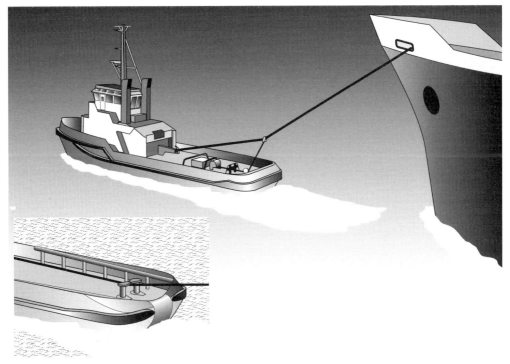

Towing fairleads

In virtually all modern tractor tugs and stern-drive vessels of any size, regardless of the type of propulsion system used, the towline passes through a very large fairlead. A large, tubular, inverted "U"-shaped structure, sometimes referred to as a "staple", is the most common form of fairlead, with a shape carefully designed to reduce the effects of chafing on the rope.

In a tractor tug the fairlead is precisely located close to the stern rail, above the underwater skeg. This has the effect of controlling the point from which the towline is effectively secured, in relation to the skeg, regardless of whether a winch or tow hook is used.

A similar fairlead, sometimes in the form of a heavy tubular "H", is fitted on the foredeck of stern-drive tugs and located just forward of the winch. Alternatively, a heavy steel fairlead is built into the centre of the forward bulwarks. Again the purpose is to provide an accurate "point of tow" and avoid chafing of the towline near the winch drum.

This picture, taken from the wheelhouse of the tractor tug Lady Sarah, *shows the importance of the large fairlead on her afterdeck. The tug has a steel wire towline and pendant with a short length of fibre rope to give some elasticity.*
(Author)

Stop pins and specialist line-handling equipment

Stop pins, sometimes known as "Norman pins" or "molgoggers", are vertical pins that can be fitted in the tug's after bulwark rail, one on each quarter. They are often used in the conventional tug to prevent the towline from passing over the sides of the vessel, particularly when the rope is being retrieved and there is a danger of its end fouling the propeller. The pins take a number of forms, the most simple being solid or tubular pins inserted in sockets in the after rail. In larger vessels they may be supported in hinged brackets, allowing them to be erected when required. Modern deep-sea tugs will have massive hydraulically operated pins controlled remotely from the wheelhouse, which rise vertically from the after bulwarks when required.

Tugs employed in specialist duties, such as anchor-handling for the offshore oil industry, are frequently fitted with rather more sophisticated devices to enable their work to be carried out safely under extremely hazardous conditions. In these vessels the crews are faced with handling heavy anchors, their chains and massive wire rope pendants, in heavy weather and sometimes extremes of temperature. In order to assist with these tasks various patented devices have been developed to mechanise much of the work carried out on the exposed afterdeck.

The line handling gear shown here at the stern of the anchor-handling rig supply vessel Punta Scario *comprises two hydraulically operated stop pins and a gripping device of the "Triplex" type. Also visible is the stern roller and timber cladding of her after deck.* (Author)

The more common consist of retractable "jaws", "stoppers", and clamping devices that can be raised from the deck to control the chains and wires used in anchor-handling operations. When not required they are lowered flush with the deck, and are operated remotely along with the controls for the winches, stop pins and other deck equipment.

The use of this type of equipment, sometimes in a simpler form, is increasingly used in powerful ship-handling tugs and escort vessels to control towing gear over the stern, and in some cases obviate the need for the gog rope. Further information is included in the section on anchor-handling tugs and oil rig supply vessels.

An alternative type of line handling equipment fitted to many anchor-handling vessels is the Karm Fork. The two forks in the foreground rise vertically from the deck to grip or control the wires or chains used in anchor-handling or towing. The associated stop pins can be raised, lowered or rotated to produce a form of closed or open fairlead. (Karmoy Winch)

Stern rollers

The use of an open stern, to enable anchors, chains and similar pieces of equipment to be hauled on to the vessel's afterdeck, is a design feature introduced originally in oil rig supply vessels and anchor-handling tugs. In order to prevent excessive damage to the stern of the vessel from these awkward objects, the extreme end of the after deck is heavily rounded or, more often than not, fitted with a large roller recessed into the deck edge. The use of stern rollers has increased considerably in recent years, with tugs of all sizes being called upon to handle moorings and hoses at offshore moorings, deploy anti-pollution booms and support civil engineering work. In most cases the rollers are parallel cylinders, with sufficient strength to resist impact damage, and are intended to rotate freely when heavy objects pass over them. The stern of the vessel, around the ends of the roller, is generally shaped to avoid sharp corners and give free passage through the stern opening.

The afterdeck of the ship-handling tug Burcht *has towbeams or protective rails over several deck fittings to prevent fouling. Her towing winch is partially enclosed. A small winch for the gog rope is located in the centre of the deck with a hinged sheave for the rope close to the after bulwarks.* (Author)

Bitts and bollards

In common with all ships and smaller craft, tugs have an obvious need for the usual mooring bitts, or bollards. These are rather stronger in construction than in many other vessels because in some of the roles the tug is called upon to perform they may be used to help secure the tow. Many tugs are fitted with a large "stem post" in the bow and similar "shoulder posts" on the port and starboard quarters. These, likewise, have multiple uses in mooring and towing.

The capstan

Possibly one of the oldest pieces of mechanised deck equipment in the shipping industry, the capstan is still alive and well in many present-day tugs. The basic concept remains unchanged: a power-driven vertical barrel with a concave outer surface, used to heave and control ropes. The modern capstan is usually driven either by an electric or hydraulic motor and operated by a simple control, conveniently located within easy reach of the user.

In tugs where no towing winch is fitted, the capstan is the most common means of retrieving or shortening a synthetic rope towline. Two or three turns of the rope around the capstan give the crew on deck assistance in getting the rope aboard easily and with a high degree of control. Where the rope is too large to pass conveniently around the capstan, a lighter "messenger" rope may be used to haul the towline on board in stages. The capstan is sometimes used in conjunction with a gog rope (see the earlier section) to control the towline, as an aid during mooring and for many other purposes.

A common alternative is to have a drum head fitted to the anchor windlass or towing winch, which can then used in the same way as a capstan. These horizontal drums are found in all types of tug and again have a wide range of uses. Many vessels, particularly in Europe, have separate powered drums located horizontally in convenient positions on the after superstructure.

Tow beams

This is the name given to the beams or guards used to prevent the towline from fouling or becoming entangled with items of equipment and fittings on the tug's afterdeck, although they are an item of equipment found less and less in modern tugs. They may take the form of guards located over individual parts of the vessel or beams that extend from bulwark to bulwark.

Deck cranes

Some form of crane or simple lifting derrick has always been an important item of equipment on tugs involved in salvage or offshore work, where the movement of heavy equipment and spares can be an everyday chore. However, the derrick has been replaced largely by the much more convenient deck crane. Such cranes are usually operated electrically or hydraulically and range in power from about 2 to 20 tons lifting capacity.

In other types of tug, smaller crews and the need to employ vessels more effectively have resulted in small hydraulic cranes being fitted on the majority of new tugs and many older ones. Such equipment is used for the transfer of stores, the launching of workboats and to assist in the maintenance of harbour facilities. Vessels involved in anti-pollution duties are likely to be fitted with a crane suitable to lift and manipulate protective booms and possibly skimming equipment. The cranes generally have telescopic jibs and, when not in use, can be folded or stowed to minimise the space they occupy.

Line-handling cranes

A number of North American tug operators use a small, specially adapted hydraulic crane to assist in the process of making a towing connection. Tugs using this equipment are small, powerful, stern-drive ship-handling tugs operating with very small crews. The line-handling crane is used to lift the end of the towline to a point level with the ship's bulwarks, where it can be easily retrieved by the ship's crew and made secure – thus avoiding the necessity of throwing heaving lines, and hauling towlines aboard manually. The crane is normally located just aft of the foredeck winch and operated directly from the wheelhouse by the tug's master.

Vancouver is a stern drive tug of 3000 bhp built for the Shaver Transportation Company and operated by 2-3 personnel. A remotely controlled line handling crane is fitted to the foredeck adjacent to the towing winch to assist in making a towing connection. Note the bow fender which comprises three heavy truck tyres on a central column. *(Robert Allan Ltd)*

CHAPTER 4

Ancillary and navigational equipment

This chapter might well have been entitled "everything else that goes to make an operational tug". Contained here are many of the items of a tug's equipment that enable it to perform safely and efficiently in providing the wide range of services associated with this type of vessel. The term "ancillary" certainly does not mean that the items mentioned are unimportant. Many of them can be found in virtually any small ship, but in tugs certain items of marine equipment are often of particular importance. Other more specialised features are fitted to improve the tug's versatility or fit it for a particular role. It is, for example, increasingly common for the master of a modern tug or oil rig supply vessel to have additional management responsibilities for the operation and maintenance

Thrax and Silex, *built in Norway in 1994, are a pair of 5386 bhp escort tugs operated by Solent Towage Ltd at the ESSO oil terminal at Fawley. They embody many of the features described in this chapter. Note the design of the wheelhouse and array of radar scanners, lights and monitors.* (Author)

of his own vessel or even a small fleet. This is likely to require additional computing and communications equipment to be installed to enable the extra workload to be handled efficiently.

Navigational equipment

The choice of navigational equipment fitted in tugs depends very much on the nature on their employment, but the availability of advanced and relatively inexpensive electronic aids has resulted in even very small vessels being fitted with quite sophisticated equipment. A compass is fitted in almost every type of tug. Magnetic compasses suffice in small locally based craft, while instruments of increasing sophistication are installed in coastal and deep-sea tugs. In sea-going vessels the equipment fitted differs little from a normal sea-going ship, and in some cases may be superior. Gyro compasses are frequently connected to an "auto-pilot" system, even in small harbour craft and multi-purpose vessels. This enables a course to be steered automatically during long passages, once the vessel's directional heading has been set.

Position-finding is often a very important matter in most aspects of towage. Accurate navigation for route planning is not the only consideration; in salvage and long-range towing it may be necessary to rendezvous with a casualty or

The captain's position, in the wheelhouse of Silex, *is surrounded not only by the engine, propulsion and winch controls but also navigational and other instrumentation. Five display screens shown (clockwise from the left), a 3cm radar, an electronic monitor of winch rope length and load, an electronic chart display, a 10 cm automatic plotting radar and a recording echo sounder. Also included are VHF and MF radios, an autopilot and two gyro compasses.* (Author)

Common items of equipment in most modern tugs of any size are a Global Positioning System (left), showing here the position, speed and heading of the Redbridge. *On the right is an echo sounder, with a colour display and a NAVTEX receiver.* (Author)

another tug well away from coastal stations and local navigational aids. The offshore oil industry also requires great accuracy when positioning oil drilling rigs, pipelines and other equipment. Traditional navigational methods and many established radio position-finding systems relying on coastal stations have been replaced or supplemented by modern satellite navigation equipment. Known as "Global Positioning Systems" (GPS), this sophisticated electronic equipment uses signals from space satellites to provide extremely accurate positional information, usually in the form of straightforward longitude and latitude figures. Such technology has advanced rapidly, hand in hand with equipment miniaturisation, to produce GPSs suitable for all types of vessel. The equipment is generally very small in size and easily installed. In addition to displays of longitude and latitude, a typical unit will give the vessel's speed, heading and make other calculations automatically. For more specialised use, systems known as "Differential Global Positioning Systems" (DGPS) have been introduced in most parts of the world to give positional accuracy down to just a few metres. DGPS relies on additional land-based stations to enhance the accuracy of the satellite data.

A recent innovation that quickly found an important place aboard many tugs and similar craft is electronic charting. Navigational and hydrographic charts of specific areas are now widely available in electronic form and can be displayed on a Visual Display Unit (VDU), and integrated with other information, usually from the vessel's GPS and/or radar. This enables the tug's position to be shown accurately on the VDU screen in real time on a detailed chart of the operational area. Additional information, such as shipping channels or search areas and the tracks of ships in the vicinity, can be superimposed on the chart to assist the tug master. Electronic charts are stored on magnetic tape and magnetic or optical discs and may be updated regularly. As yet, maritime regulations do not allow these systems to replace traditional paper charts completely, but it is known that systems are becoming available with suitable built-in safeguards to satisfy international standards.

Echo sounder

Accurate depth-finding is also an important need in every tug. Because of the nature of their work, tugs probably spend more time in coastal waters than most other vessels; they are often required to work close inshore on civil engineering projects or manoeuvre to assist ships aground, operations that demand an accurate knowledge of the depth of water and the profile of the seabed or river bottom. Practically every tug is equipped with at least one echo sounder, an instrument that uses sound waves to measure the distance between the keel of the tug and the ground; this is a universal method of depth measurement used throughout the shipping industry. Modern equipment is available that can read depth to within a few centimetres. Many tugs and oil rig supply vessels are fitted with instruments that show the information on a colour graphic display and produce a recording of the depth measurements and seabed profile in the form of a chart.

Radar

Radar has proved invaluable in tugs, where it has several different roles. The most obvious application is in navigation in the dark and in poor weather conditions, particularly in coastal waters and busy shipping lanes. In this role it is possible to locate accurately other vessels and various features of the shoreline. In common with many similar pieces of electronic equipment, the modern radar set has advanced enormously in recent years. A typical modern radar, installed in a harbour or coastal tug, will have a high-definition colour display screen and many features enabling range to be measured and possible hazards to be plotted automatically. The range will be adjustable, depending on the type of set, between perhaps 0.5 and 36 nautical miles, with a maximum range of 72 miles. Two and even three separate radars may be fitted in larger tugs; this would enable, for example, one set to be used at very short range, monitoring possible hazards nearby, and another to be adjusted to a longer range for navigational purposes. As previously mentioned, data from a radar set may be integrated with an electronic chart display to superimpose additional information, such as the position of other vessels, on to the electronic chart.

In salvage work the radar set has transformed the whole business of locating ships in trouble. Used in conjunction with modern navigational aids and communications equipment, searching is no longer the lengthy, tedious procedure it was in the early days before radar was invented. If a towline breaks in very bad weather conditions, providing there is no hazardous shoreline nearby, the tug may well make no attempt to reconnect until conditions improve. The tow will be monitored at a safe distance using radar and, if necessary, warnings broadcast to prevent collisions with other shipping.

Where two similar radars are fitted, as here in the Portgarth, *they are normally used with different range settings. In this picture the vessel is lying in the corner of a dock with the radars set to ranges of 0.5 and 1.5 nautical miles.* (Author)

Communications equipment

The world of marine communications equipment continues to become wider and more complex. Advances in communications technology and the increased use of space satellites in particular have completely changed many aspects of radio communication between ships, and ship-to-shore links. Facilities now available to even very small vessels have a profound effect on the way that tugs can be operated and managed.

Even the smallest tug and workboat is equipped with a VHF (Very High Frequency) radio telephone to enable the vessel to communicate easily with her owners, port authorities, and other shipping. In most ports throughout the world the VHF radio telephone has replaced whistle signals and hooters as the main means of communication between tug captains, ships' masters and pilots during ship-handling operations. The use of synthesised electronic channel selection circuitry has made such radio equipment extremely versatile; a very small radio set will often be capable of operating on all 80 channels in the international VHF marine band. This frequency band is intended for relatively short-range use; depending on the equipment and local geography conditions, 20 to 30 miles is normally regarded as the maximum range. Radios of this kind are standard equipment on all larger tugs for ship-to-ship and ship-to-shore use. Very often two or more sets are fitted to enable several functions to be carried out at the same time. A common facility on this type of radio telephone is known as a "dual watch", which allows the international distress and calling channel, channel 16, to be monitored regardless of other activities.

For longer-range use, standard HF (High Frequency) and MF (Medium Frequency) radios are used, operating in the international marine bands. Radio equipment of this type is fitted in most sea-going tugs and has for many years been the standard method of communication between ships, owners and agents, often working through the national coastal radio stations. The HF band also has designated distress frequencies, which are monitored not only by the various rescue authorities and shipping in general but also by towage and salvage concerns.

Much of the communications traffic between ships, tugs and other craft, their owners and other land-based agencies, now passes over satellite radio communications systems. As with other shipborne electronics equipment, such systems are rapidly coming within the means of most operators of sea-going vessels. The main advantage offered by radio systems of this kind is the worldwide coverage possible, via the satellite link, without the need for complicated land-based relay arrangements. This is of particular value when the vessel is operating in remote parts of the world or involved in long ocean voyages. The facilities offered by satellite communications systems such as Inmarsat-A and B are direct-dial voice telephone, facsimile, telex and data transmission. The smaller, lightweight Inmarsat-C equipment provides "none voice" text and data transmission. Vessels equipped with satellite communications equipment are fitted with a dome or a conical-shaped antenna, located on the mast or high above the wheelhouse.

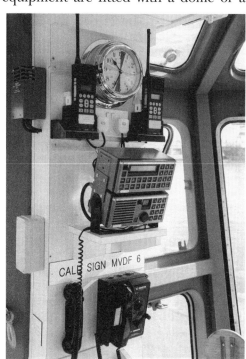

Such systems have become an important ingredient in initiatives to improve maritime safety. A recent innovation is the Global Maritime Distress and Safety System (GMDSS), developed by the International Maritime Organisation (IMO) and recognised worldwide. International regulations require the implementation of GMDSS, which will eventually affect all vessels over 300 gross tons. The GMDSS system requires a vessel to carry communications equipment capable of meeting certain standards for the sea area in which it will operate, with respect to radio communications and search and rescue facilities.

In addition to various radio communications equipment of the types previously mentioned, vessels are also required to carry Emergency Position Indicating Radio Beacons (EPIRBs) and Search and Rescue Radar Transponders (SARTs). EPIRBs are radio beacons carried aboard the parent vessel and in lifeboats or rafts, which, when activated, alert the satellite communications system to the vessel's current position. One form of EPIRB is incorporated in a buoy that floats

Under GMDSS regulations a tug is required to carry communications equipment to a certain standard (depending on size and area of operations), including portable VHF rados for immediate emergency use and a ship's VHF radio incorporating Digital Selective Calling (DSC) on distress frequencies. The fixed radios in Redbridge are Sailor VHF, shown above a sound powered telephone for internal communication. (Author)

free from a sinking vessel, remains tethered and continues to transmit a signal to mark the position of the casualty. A SART is an active radar transponder that operates in much the same manner to enhance the signal received by the radar aboard a searching vessel, giving a clearer indication of the position of the casualty, wreck or liferaft.

A further mandatory requirement for vessels over 300 gross tons is the fitting of NAVTEX equipment. NAVTEX is generally described as "receiving, automatically, Maritime Safety Information on 518 KHz, by narrow band direct printing". The equipment is rather like a very small facsimile machine, which receives a variety of information automatically at regular intervals, depending on the requirements of the operator, but always includes regular weather reports for the area of operations. Other available information can include ice reports, maritime distress warnings and notices to mariners regarding known potential hazards.

The use of facsimile transmission, and previously Telex, over radio has spread rapidly in the towage industry. It is an ideal means of transmitting and receiving charts, weather maps, technical information, drawings, contracts and other management information. The possibilities this presents to the towage and salvage operator are immense, with important documents being transmitted directly from owners and agents' offices to tugs at sea conducting towage, salvage, or offshore operations.

The land-based cellular mobile telephone has also found an important place aboard the modern tug. Although its use is obviously restricted to the more civilised and densely populated areas of the world, this type of telephone now appears in the wheelhouses of most tugs. Owners are finding such systems a convenient and relatively secure means of communicating with vessels in coastal waters, and business can be conducted in conditions of some privacy without broadcasting on international frequencies or resorting to encryption.

Lights and shapes

In general, the lights required by maritime law for navigational purposes are the same for tugs as for other shipping. There are, however, special conditions and requirements that affect tugs when they are towing. As in general shipping, there are also day marks, or shapes, which are displayed for the same purpose during daylight hours.

Towing lights and shapes

To the uninitiated, the mast of a tug seems to carry an over-abundance of lights. The vertical array fitted to the mast is a combination of towing and navigation lights; the former are illuminated in a particular order to indicate to other shipping that the tug is towing and to give some indication as to the nature of the tow. The regulations governing lights are revised from time to time but the following basic rules applied at the time of writing:

a) Tugs below 50 metres in length need only one masthead steaming light. Larger vessels exceeding that length require two steaming lights, on separate masts, in the same way as a conventional ship.

b) A tug with a tow of less than 200 metres in length, from the stern of the tug to

The Belgian stern drive tug Hemiksem *(1985 – 3600 bhp) is carrying the basic navigation and towing lights required by a ship-handling vessel of her type. Note the red, white, red lights are separated from the mast on brackets for all round visibility. Two searchlights and a compass are fitted on the wheelhouse roof and life rafts carried forward of the bridge windows.* (Author)

the stern of the tow, must carry one additional white towing light at the forward mast 2 metres below the steaming light. A tug with a tow of over 200 metres in length must show two additional towing lights.

c) A tug with a tow must show a yellow towing light aft, above her stern light.

d) Three other lights are fitted at the mast of most modern tugs. These are two red lights, arranged vertically, separated by a white light. This is the international signal for "vessels restricted in ability to manoeuvre" and is often used by a tug at sea with a tow. The lights must be visible from all round the vessel and on many tugs are mounted on brackets to separate them from the mast.

Tugs of the tractor or push-tow type, which are capable of operating equally well stern-first, may have two sets of towing and navigation lights fitted, the second set being positioned for use when the vessel is operating stern-first.

During daylight hours a black diamond shape is hoisted to the mast of a tug with a tow exceeding 200 metres in length. The red-white-red light "vessels restricted in ability to manoeuvre" signal is replaced in daylight by two black ball shapes separated by a black diamond.

Portable lights are usually provided aboard tugs, to be installed temporarily on vessels in tow that have no lights of their own. These may be powered by gas cylinders or electric batteries.

In some ports and inland waterways local bylaws require special signals to be displayed indicating when a tug is operating with a tow. These are usually flag signals or shapes, hoisted on a small additional mast.

Searchlights
Powerful searchlights are an important part of the tug's equipment, and almost every type of tug will have one or more. They have many uses: during towing operations a searchlight is used to keep a visual check on the condition of the towline and the vessel in tow, and can also be useful to identify any likely hazards located close at hand by radar. Searchlights and floodlighting are also used extensively during salvage and offshore operations to enable work to proceed around the clock.

Boats and life-saving equipment
The type of boat carried aboard tugs has changed drastically in the past 20 years. Rigid, full-size lifeboats, once common on tugs of most types, are now rarely seen aboard anything but the largest vessels. Rigid boats carried on tugs engaged in ship-handling work are a particular nuisance, are difficult to stow without impairing the vision from the wheelhouse, and are easily damaged when the tug is working close alongside a ship. Most owners throughout the world were quick to dispense with them once a suitable alternative evolved, and the vast improvements made in inflatable liferafts and the durable, semi-rigid rubber boat have been responsible for sealing the fate of the conventional boat. A modern semi-rigid is most commonly carried as a rescue craft and can be utilised as a general-purpose tender when required. A simple single-arm davit, or the tug's hydraulic crane, is used to launch and recover the boat.

Bugsier 16 is a Voith Schneider tractor tug of 3060 bhp, built for Bugsier Reederei of Hamburg in 1991, and used for ship-handling and coastal towing. Her towing lights are duplicated to allow stern first operation. An inflatable rescue boat and davit are carried forward of her wheelhouse.   (Hitzler)

Liferafts and other aids

For life-saving purposes the inflatable liferaft, stowed on deck in a sealed container, has proved to be highly convenient for a number of reasons: the space required for stowage is insignificant, and if necessary the number of rafts provided can be increased without difficulty. A single modern liferaft can easily accommodate the entire crew of all but the very largest of tugs. The liferaft container is usually stowed in a cradle incorporating a hydrostatic pressure-sensing mechanism that will release it automatically should the tug sink.

Among the other life-saving aids provided are traditional lifebuoys, distress flares, marker floats and position-indicating devices such as EPIRBs and SARTs, mentioned earlier in this chapter. A growing number of harbour craft now carry recovery devices, designed to enable personnel to be recovered from the water without the need to lower a boat. These take the form of slings, scoops or sophisticated ladder devices operated from a small davit or, again, a hydraulic crane.

Workboats

Boats are frequently needed for purposes other than life-saving. In earlier days the rigid lifeboat often doubled as a workboat, which is often necessary to collect stores, transfer personnel, put towlines aboard other vessels, and many similar tasks. More often than not those duties are now undertaken by inflatable rubber workboats, powered by outboard motors. Such boats are durable, light to handle, and with suitable engines can be quite fast. The larger versions of the semi-rigid type have a reinforced plastic lower hull and possibly an inboard engine; this type of boat is easy to stow, launch and recover. Very large sea-going and salvage tugs are still equipped with rigid boats. These may take the form of lifeboats, but in general they are intended to operate as workboats and have diesel engines sufficiently powerful to cope with difficult sea conditions and handle heavy equipment during salvage operations.

Salvage equipment

Almost every tug carries some items that come under the heading of salvage equipment; even the smallest barge tug will probably have some additional pumping equipment on board to enable her to pump out or refloat flooded barges. The amount of

This view from the bridge of the salvage tug Fotiy Krylov *shows three of the boats carried in addition to her lifeboats – a fast inflatable and two sturdy firebreglass workboats. Also in the picture are her two large deck cranes and storage reels for hoses and spare towing gear.*

(Author)

equipment carried will again depend on the type of tug and her employment. Salvage is a very wide subject on which much has been written; in the following paragraphs it is intended only to outline the basic equipment deployed for salvage work. With the number of dedicated salvage tugs falling, many salvage specialists store and maintain salvage equipment in a form that can be quickly mobilised and put aboard any suitable tug or oil rig supply vessel capable of attending a casualty. Many of the items mentioned here fall into that category and will be sufficiently portable to allow them to be transported by air to any part of the world.

Salvage pumps
Additional pumping equipment is one of the most common facilities provided, and usually takes the form of high-capacity pumps fitted to the tug's auxiliary machinery. The diesel-driven generators, air compressors and other auxiliaries located in the engine room often have a salvage pump fitted that can be engaged when required. Such pumps are piped to connections, easily accessible, on deck, to which suction hoses can be fitted. The purpose-built pumps fitted for salvage work are capable of moving water at an extremely high rate; capacities of well in excess of 100 tonnes per hour are not uncommon.

Additional portable salvage pumps are carried aboard tugs operating regularly in salvage, or may be supplied from specialists ashore. These are usually diesel-driven, self-contained units or submersible pumps driven by an electrical or air supply. Diesel pumps are stowed aboard the salvage tug and can be lifted on to the deck of a casualty if the necessity arises. Submersible pumps are designed to be lowered into the flooded areas of a casualty, connected to a hose. A common type of submersible pump popular on tugs is one driven by high-pressure water. There are no electrical hazards involved and a suitable water supply is readily available on most vessels.

Air and electrical supplies
There are frequently heavy demands for compressed air and electrical supplies during a salvage operation. Again, the systems aboard many tugs are geared to some degree to provide external supplies of electricity and sometimes compressed air. The uses of electricity in salvage are easy to comprehend: lighting, portable tools, pumping, and welding equipment frequently require power from the parent tug. The use of compressed air to aid the refloating of badly damaged vessels has been popular with the salvage experts for many years. Power tools increasingly use compressed air as a source of power, a much safer medium than electricity in a marine environment. There remain many steam-driven ships in use throughout the world, and these often have a large amount of steam-driven equipment that is unusable if for some reason the boilers are out of action. Even simple actions such as raising anchors are then impossible. The only alternative most present-day tugs can provide is compressed air, which is quite effective in most circumstances. It may be impractical to supply electricity or compressed air from the tug's own systems; large sea-going salvage tugs carry portable diesel-powered generators and compressors on board, or alternatively they may be acquired from facilities ashore.

Anchors and ground tackle

Among the most common items found aboard a large sea-going or salvage tug are additional anchors. These are generally somewhat heavier than the vessel's own anchors and may well be of a special design. Additional anchors are used to assist with the refloating of vessels that have gone aground. They may be incorporated in ground tackle, very heavy multiple-pulley systems rigged to exert a much greater pull than would be possible by towing alone.

Line-throwing equipment

Most tugs, of any size, have on board some means of getting a light heaving line to vessels that for some reason cannot be approached too closely. If a ship is aground in shallow water, or if the weather is exceptionally bad, the tug will not be able to manoeuvre alongside in the normal way. The most common method of making a towing connection under these circumstances is to fire a light line over the vessel by rocket or line-throwing gun. Once contact is made in this way, heavier lines and eventually a towline can be hauled aboard the casualty and made fast. Line-throwing equipment varies from simple expendable rockets, which give one attempt, to guns that can be reloaded with fresh projectiles and line.

Underwater equipment

There is an obvious need aboard a salvage tug for some form of diving capability. In larger vessels this may be part of the tug's equipment, or alternatively provision may be made to accommodate specialist gear and personnel when required. The range of equipment carried can again vary enormously, from simple scuba-diving gear to full-scale deep-diving outfits with a decompression chamber provided on board.

Included under this heading is equipment for cutting and welding and the means of carrying out other repair work underwater. Special tools are available for use underwater, such as spanners, drills and hammers driven by compressed air. Some provision may also be made for the storage and use of explosives; these are used in salvage work for cutting purposes, to disperse wreckage and blast away rock.

Fire-fighting equipment

Fire-fighting equipment of some kind is installed on board virtually every tug. This capability usually extends beyond that needed to protect the vessel herself from fires on board, and the equipment fitted ranges from the provision of a few hose connections and extinguishers to sophisticated installations capable of undertaking important fire-protection duties. Specialist fire-fighting tugs, their equipment and duties are described in a later chapter, so the following paragraphs deal with the more common and less specialised installations.

Fire mains and hoses

The term "fire main" refers to a water supply, generally provided by a powerful pump in the engine room, which can be used to fight fires on board or to assist another vessel. A fire pump can be driven by one of the auxiliary engines or, in some tugs, by the main engine. The fire main is a system of pipes routed to deliver a supply of water to hose connections within the vessel and on deck. Hoses are attached to these connections and may be fitted with suitable nozzles for fire-fighting. In most vessels the fire main is identified from the mass of other pipework by being painted red.

Monitors
Because of the difficulty in accurately directing high-pressure jets of water during fire-fighting operations, some form of nozzle, fixed to the structure of the vessel, is often used. These are known as monitors, and in their simplest form are nozzles located on a mounting designed to enable water jets be controlled with some accuracy. This is usually achieved by a system of handwheels and simple gear mechanisms. In the more sophisticated installations the monitor will be capable of delivering either water or a water/foam mixture. The output from a high-performance fire monitor can vary from approximately 1,500 to as much as 60,000 litres of water per minute. If fire-fighting foam is used, the chemical compound needed is introduced into the water supply, prior to the monitor, from storage tanks installed on board. When foam is in use the volume delivered by the monitor is considerably higher than with water alone.

Far Turbot *is typical of many anchor-handling oil rig supply vessels equipped for standby and emergency response duties. As a vessel of over 50 metres in length she carries an additional forward mast to carry the mandatory lights. High capacity fire monitors are fitted on a gantry between the exhaust uptakes.* (Author)

CHAPTER 5

Small tugs and multi-purpose vessels

Small tugs are by their very nature the most prolific and diverse vessels in the towing business in terms of employment and design. In many small commercial ports they are the veritable "maids of all work", assisting small ships, working with barges and dredgers and being involved in many of the routine maintenance tasks. A great many small tugs are employed by towage contractors specialising in supporting civil engineering work in harbours and at riverside locations. It is common for such vessels to be owned by very small companies or owner-operators, often working on a contract basis for individual jobs or hired regularly to perform a particular towage operation. Some undertake long journeys to fulfil contracts in other ports and sometimes other countries. A great many small tugs currently operated in this way were formerly part of major tug company fleets and were sold off when they became too small, or outmoded. Included in this "small tug" category are the growing numbers of multi-purpose vessels capable of towing, pushing and many other services previously carried out by small traditional tugs. Many small modern tugs and multi-purpose vessels are particularly suitable for mass or series production. This has resulted in a proliferation of proprietary "standard" vessels being purchased to undertake many of the duties described in this chapter.

There are many small vessels that regularly give assistance to other craft by towing or pushing, but are excluded here because towing is very much a supplementary duty. Workboats, passenger launches, construction vessels and even pilot cutters often have some provision for securing a towrope and, when needed, undertake small towing jobs, but cannot be regarded as tugs. For the purposes of this chapter the starting point will be the small tug/workboat of some 20 gross tons and larger.

Traditional barge tugs
Barge tugs of traditional design are still widely used on inland waterways where barge trades have survived. Europe has a large population of such craft operating in Holland, Belgium, France and Germany, though many have been adapted to push their barges. In Britain very few have remained in their traditional trade, but a great number have found alternative employment as small harbour tugs and contracting vessels. The term "barge tug" in the USA can mean a small craft, similar to those used in Europe, or a very much larger vessel used on major waterways or in coastal operations. In this chapter we shall deal only with the towing tug – in Europe and

Guy James *is one of many small vessels of the tug/workboat type regularly engaged in ship-handling and other port services. Built by the Damen Shipyard in Gorinchem for James Butcher & Sons Ltd of Portsmouth in 1995, she is a twin-screw vessel of 16.9 metres in length powered by Caterpillar engines of 940 bhp.* (Author)

Today's Tugs in Colour

The small twin-screw tug Zwerver I *was built in 1994 for Hans van Stee Sleepdienst of Harlingen, and specially equipped to support dredging and civil engineering work. She is 22 metres in length and powered by Cummins engines of 1,014 bhp. Fixed Kort nozzles are fitted to give her a bollard pull of 12 tonnes, and a bow thruster to enhance manoeuvrability.* (Author)

Koos Bay Tow Boat Company of Oregon took delivery of the compact stern-drive tug Tioga *from builders Tri-Star Marine in 1994. Designed to operate efficiently with a small crew, she is a well-equipped vessel of 25.9 metres in length powered by two Caterpillar engines producing 4,000 bhp and a bollard pull of 48 tonnes.*   (Ship & Boat Int)

The stern-drive tug John *is seen here working with other tugs of the Roda Bolaget tug fleet to berth the tanker* Alandia Trader *at the Gothenburg crude oil terminal. The 4,000 bhp* John *is secured at the stern of the ship with the towline from her forward winch to enable her to assist with slowing and steering the vessel.*   (Roda Bolaget)

A typical ship-handling operation in Europort, Holland. The 2,400 bhp twin-screw tug Smit
Polen *is working on the head of a tanker. Built in 1986, she is a vessel of 28.6 metres and 236
gross tons with a bollard pull of 35 tonnes. The vessel in the background is sister ship* Smit Japan,
also owned by the Smit Harbour Towage Co. (Author)

Medway tugs Lady Morag *and* Lady Brenda *demonstrate the ability of stern-drive tugs to work
effectively towing astern while berthing the cargo ship* Kudu. Lady Morag, *in the foreground, is a
vessel of 36.3 metres in length and 3,400 bhp, built in Yokohama in 1983.* (Author)

Boss *and sister vessel* Bess *are unique among Voith Schneider tractor tugs. Owned by Roda Bolaget, they are tugs of 5,460 bhp optimised in every respect to run with the skeg end of the vessel forward, giving excellent performance in the escort role. The tug, built in 1995, has a bollard pull of 57 tonnes and a free running speed of 15 knots.* (Roda Bolaget)

Garth Foss *is one of a pair of massive Voith tractor tugs built for Foss Maritime of Seattle in 1994 to provide tanker escort services in the Strait of Juan de Fuca and Puget Sound. Like her sister ship* Lindsey Foss *she is a vessel of 47.25 metres in length and 475 gross tons, powered by main engines of some 8,000 bhp. The tugs have a bollard pull of over 70 tonnes and a speed of 14.5 knots.* (Foss)

Many tanker-handling and escort tugs are also equipped to act as emergency response vessels in the event of a major pollution incident. Thorax, built for Johannes Ostensjo of Haugesund in 1993, is a very powerful example. She is a stern-drive vessel of 45.5 metres in length and 7,180 bhp, with a bollard pull of 90 tonnes. (Johannes Ostensjo)

The fire-fighting tug Fiery Cross, from the fleet of Cory Towage Ltd of Middlesbrough, demonstrates the power of her remotely operated monitors. Fire pumps driven by both main engines deliver a total of 1,450 cubic metres of water per hour to the monitors and the vessel's self-protection system. Fiery Cross is a Voith Schneider tractor built in 1993 and equipped to the Fi Fi 1 standard. (Ray Johnson)

Stella Wind, *built for the Cook Inlet Tug & Barge Company of Anchorage, Alaska, by Tri-Star Marine of Seattle in 1994 is a stern-drive tug strengthened to operate in the icy conditions of the west coast of North America. The 25.9-metre tug has main engines producing a total of 3,000 bhp.*
(Ship & Boat Int)

The deep-sea tug Solano *is seen here leaving Holland with a "dry tow" bound for Shanghai in China, via the Suez Canal. The submersible barge* AMT Transporter, *owned by Anchor Marine Services, is loaded with a whole fleet of vessels for dredging and civil engineering work, including cranes, barges and small tugs.* *(ITC)*

Oil rig supply vessels, such as the Normand Jarl *shown here, are increasingly required to operate in extreme climatic conditions as the search for oil offshore continues.* Normand Jarl *is an anchor-handling oil rig supply vessel of 1,485 gross tons and 12,000 bhp, built in 1984 for Solstad Offshore A/S of Norway. She is also fully equipped for fire-fighting and stand-by duties.* (Ulstein)

Morania No 3 *is typical of many America tugs operating in the barge trades. She is a twin-screw tug of 36.63 metres in length built in 1973 and powered by two General Motors main engines producing 3,900 bhp. Note the additional high-level wheelhouse for use when pushing, and a further control position on the after end of the boat deck.* (Michael Vincent)

Pusher tugs and their tows travel long distances on the inland waterways of Europe. Hammonia *is typical of many medium-sized vessels. Note the folding masts and radar scanners, well-glazed wheelhouse and extensive accommodation.* (Author)

The small pusher tug Envoy, *of Mon River Towing Inc of Belle Vernon, Pennsylvania, USA, is depicted working with loaded coal barges. Built in 1965, she is a twin-screw vessel of 19.8 metres in length and 760 bhp used mainly for short journeys and preparing tows for larger towboats.* (Lawrence Amboldt)

Ayrenco is a small traditional Thames launch tug built in 1928 and now sports a 120 bhp Meadows diesel engine. She is owned by J R Waterage and seen here working with barges in London's Limehouse Basin. (Author)

America tugs of this type, size and power are often equipped to push and tow. Examples of these are included in a later chapter on pusher tugs.

The smallest of the traditional barge tugs is the "launch tug" or "tosher", terms that describe a very small tug of a traditional design used mainly to handle single barges or other small craft. Originally intended for use in the barge and lighterage industries, several of these craft remain in service in Britain and elsewhere. Few tugs of this type were built after the mid-1960s, but they remained popular due to their sturdy construction, rounded hull form and low profile. An average launch tug will have a length of some 12 to 15 metres and a gross tonnage of about 20 tons. They are generally single-screw vessels powered by a diesel engine of 125–400 bhp housed in an engine room taking up most of the space within the hull.

The launch tug was originally developed to handle barges singly or in small numbers and marshal such craft in readiness for larger tugs to undertake the longer journeys. To that end the hull is strongly built to withstand hard use, and the low profile enables the craft to proceed under river and dock bridges without the need for them to be raised or opened. Some barge companies still employ these vessels for their original purpose, but in many applications they are being replaced by more modern tug/workboats of similar size and power.

Like their smaller sisters, the larger traditional barge tugs are invariably strongly built to withstand heavy contact with their charges. A feature that often identifies them from a ship-handling tug of the same size is the bulwarks, which are generally tailored to provide some protection, yet low enough to avoid fouling towropes or sustain undue damage from contact with barges. In size, most British and European barge tugs will be less than 100 tons gross and 24 metres in overall length. They are fitted with a single conventional screw propeller; twin screws were avoided by many owners because the propeller blades can be easily damaged by contact with barges. The main engine will be a diesel of between 350 and 1,000 bhp; their larger American cousins are often considerably more powerful than this. In modern vessels a gearbox will be installed, but a number of direct reversing diesel engine installations are still in use. The engine and gearbox will be controlled from the wheelhouse and most engine rooms will be capable of being left unattended for long periods. Kort nozzles are used by some owners and may be of the fixed or steerable type. Many older barge tugs have been fitted with nozzles to improve their performance, a fixed nozzle being the most likely choice. On European waterways the modern "standard" tug has replaced many of the smaller traditional craft. Vessels of the tug/workboat type, with main engines of 750–1,000 bhp, excellent handling characteristics and good accommodation for a small crew, will often be seen working with barges in Holland and Belgium in much the same way as their earlier counterparts.

The methods used to handle barges depend on the type and size of barge and the conditions on the waterway concerned. On some waterways the total length of the tug and her tow are governed by local bylaws. Barges towed astern may be arranged in "strings", two or three long and two or more abreast. On the River Thames, for example, a string of barges of 250 tons each, three long and two abreast, was commonplace when the lighterage industry was thriving. Such tows still continue, but the cargoes are mainly domestic rubbish for disposal or materials for building purposes. The tendency now is to use fewer but larger

The barge tug Mamba *is operated by Alan C. Bennett and Sons of Rochester in Kent, specialists in the transportation of bulk materials.* Mamba, *a single screw vessel built in 1961 and fitted with a 1000 bhp British Polar main engine, is towing a 1000 ton barge loaded with excavated spoil.* (Author)

Indus is typical of many small traditional tugs in used throughout north west Europe. She is a vessel of 108 gross tons with a 890 bhp MAN main engine, originally built in 1964. The vessel is owned by the Dutch towage contractor H Hubregtse of Scharendijke. (Author)

barges. When operating on tidal waterways, journeys are timed to make the maximum use of any advantage that can be gained from the flow of the tides.

In Europe and the USA barges are generally very much larger and used mainly for bulk and containerised cargoes. Single barges are often towed with the tug secured alongside and positioned very near to the stern of the barge. This arrangement enables the tug and barge to be controlled very much as one vessel and is particularly useful with light craft, which sometimes tow badly astern. In both regions, pushing from astern is the most popular means of handling barges over long distances on inland waterways.

Standard tugs and tug/workboats

Whole ranges of standard vessels have evolved and are marketed, mainly from Holland, to replace many of the older tugs employed by small harbour authorities, dredging concerns, and civil engineers. Although often referred to as tug/workboats, they are regarded as true tugs by the majority of owners. To many of the older tugmen they resemble large motor launches rather than true tugs, but their many advantages have made them a very popular product. A number of sizes are available, normally from about 12 to 22 metres in length. For the uses mentioned a 15-metre version, of some 40 gross tons, is very common. Most are twin-screw and commonly powered by a pair of diesel engines producing a total of about 850 bhp. Kort nozzles are fitted if required and generally a vessel of this type and size will produce a bollard pull of about 11 tons. A large wheelhouse is provided and sufficient accommodation for a crew of two or three. A small "flying bridge" with duplicated engine and steering controls is sometimes fitted to give improved all-round vision.

Such vessels are extremely manoeuvrable and have sufficient power to carry out a very wide range of duties extremely economically. They are used in many smaller ports to assist ships and provide many other supporting services. The dredging

The tug/workboat Gray Vixen *is seen assisting the barge carrier* Spruce *from her berth at Felixstowe.* Gray Vixen *was built by the Delta Shipyard in Sliedrecht, Holland in 1991 to a standard 16.5 metre design for Felixarc Marine Ltd. Two Cummins main engines produce a total of 850 bhp to give her a 11 ton bollard pull.* (Author)

Zephyr *is one of several small Voith Schneider tractors built, in 1964, to the same design as a series of similar vessels for the British navy. She is powered by a single propulsion unit driven by Lister Blackstone main engine of 330 bhp.* Zephyr *has been modernised by her owners the Spithead Trading Company to support marine civil engineering work.* (Author)

industry was one of the first serious commercial users of these modern standard vessels. They have proved ideal tugs to handle the hopper barges used to take spoil away for dumping and to assist with the repositioning of dredging plant.

Where bigger and more powerful tugs are required, suitable vessels are available from the ranges offered. In the small tug category a number of compact designs are employed, up to about 2,000 bhp. In general these follow closely the designs used for larger ship-handling and coastal tugs, but scaled down for a particular purpose. These are often employed as small ship-handling tugs or to carry out more specialised duties. Larger pieces of plant, such as floating cranes, are regularly attended by small twin-screw tugs that are powerful enough to attend them at sea if necessary.

Tractor tugs

From the inception of the tractor tug concept there was a perceived need for small vessels of this type. The ability to manoeuvre in any direction with great precision has obvious advantages, particularly when handling awkward craft in very confined spaces. Voith Schneider propulsion systems have been successfully applied to many quite small tractor tugs designed to carry out just this type of operation. Several tug companies in Britain, Holland, Belgium and France introduced such vessels very successfully to handle small ships, barges and floating construction plant. A dozen very small Voith Schneider tractors were built for service with the British Ministry of Defence (Navy) and are typical of many others. They are only 18 metres in length, each with a single propulsion unit driven by a 330 bhp diesel engine, and are used extensively in naval bases and dockyards to work with the many barges and non-propelled craft used to service warships. Originally developed from a commercial design dating back to 1964, they have been particularly successful. In Europe tugs of a similar size are in use, but embody twin propulsion units, thus considerably enhancing their agility and handling characteristics in difficult situations. Tugs of this type are particularly useful in docking and undocking vessels at dry docks and slipways. The civil engineering industry sometimes has the need to position structures very accurately – for instance, bridge components, piers, and lock gates – and small tractor tugs are frequently used in these operations. Secured alongside the lifting craft or supporting barges, they are able to use their directional thrust to control precisely the position of the vessels.

Many such vessels remain in use but very few small tractor tugs have been built in recent years. The relatively high capital costs involved in fitting sophisticated propulsion units and the increasing popularity of advanced twin-screw designs appear to have turned the tide against them.

The multi-purpose work vessel

An increasingly popular and relative newcomer to the towage industry is the multi-purpose work vessel. Often referred to as a "multi-cat", this is a vessel resembling a small pusher tug with a long open foredeck. The hull is normally a simple rectangular pontoon shape, housing two engines and a conventional twin-screw propulsion system. A typical example would be powered by diesel engines with a total power output of 750–1,000 bhp. Fixed Kort propulsion nozzles are

The "Multi-cat" Voe Venture *is one of a growing breed of versatile multi-purpose work vessels. Seen here loading spare parts for a dredging pipeline directly from the beach, she is a twin screw vessel of 18.42 metres in length and 900 bhp owned by Delta Marine Services of Lerwick in the Shetland Islands.* (Author)

often fitted and the vessel would have a useful bollard pull of some 10–15 tons. Push knees are located at the bow and a small wheelhouse at the stern.

A towing hook or bollard is installed aft and a powerful winch amidships; the latter is used mainly to support lifting operations and anchor-handling over the bow of the vessel. To facilitate this a bow roller is fitted at deck level between the push knees. The open foredeck is used as a working and cargo area, and a small hydraulic crane is usually installed. Because of their rectangular pontoon shape, the vessels have a shallow draught and a large reserve of buoyancy, making them ideal for load-carrying and lifting. The result is a powerful multi-purpose craft capable of working with construction barges and carrying out a wide range of towing and other duties. Such vessels are employed mainly by companies specialising in work for the civil engineering industry and harbour authorities.

The employment of small tugs
The duties of the harbour tug and barge-towing vessel are perhaps obvious, but there are many forms of employment for the small tug that are more specialised and worthy of further description.

Port services
In ports where one small tug is the only harbour craft of any size and power and perhaps manned by a regular crew, she may have to perform a wide range of duties in addition to giving towage assistance to ships. A common task placed upon the harbour tug is the maintenance of buoys and channel markers of

various kinds in use around the port. This work will vary from routine maintenance, requiring only the servicing of lights and equipment in situ, to towing a complete buoy into port. In order to carry out this type of operation some means of lifting is needed to deal with the heavy "sinker" or anchor keeping the buoy in place. A lifting sheave (pulley) in the bow or a stern roller may be used, or a small crane may be fitted. A larger harbour tug carrying out this work may even take an entire buoy on to her afterdeck. The port tug may also be used to assist with dredging operations and/or raking, as described later in this chapter.

Another duty frequently falling to the small harbour tug is the transportation of pilots and personnel to and from ships at anchor or in transit. Where this is a regular duty the tug may be required to conform to local regulations regarding the carriage of passengers; this generally involves the provision of additional safety equipment and an upper limit on the number of passengers allowed. Going alongside ships to put pilots aboard can be a hazardous business while they are under way, particularly in poor weather. Although the tug may be well fendered and equipped to do this work, additional hand-rails are often fitted for the safety of personnel transferring between vessels.

The navies of the world are well versed in the use of small tugs in large numbers at dockyards and around naval bases to handle the smaller types of warship, barges, fuel lighters and similar vessels. Many navies employ "off the shelf" standard tugs with little modification, while others may develop their own designs in order to cope with special conditions and needs. They may have conventional screw propulsion or employ systems giving superior manoeuvrability.

The twin screw tug Wyeforce *is owned by Itchen Marine Services Ltd, a company providing towage and other port services in Southampton. She is a vessel of 57 gross tons built by the Hepworth Shipyard of Hull in 1993. Two Cummins engines of 1348 bhp (total) drive fixed pitch propellers in Kort nozzles to give a bollard pull of 18.3 tons.* (Author)

Line-handling tugs

Craft known as line-handling tugs or mooring vessels are widely used to assist with the mooring of large tankers at oil terminals, handling the heavy mooring ropes during berthing operations, and towing them away from the ship to the jetty or adjacent mooring dolphins. At terminals where the tankers are required to moor at buoys, mooring vessels are required to make the ship fast to the buoy while ship-handling tugs hold it in position. Where tankers load or unload at special mooring buoys it may also be the task of the mooring vessels to tow floating hoses into position so that the necessary connections can be made. The same craft are often part of an anti-pollution organisation stationed at the tanker terminal and will be used to tow protective booms into place, either as a precautionary measure or if an oil spill occurs.

In order to carry out these duties satisfactorily, many such vessels are based on established tug designs. They must have sufficient power to handle the heavy gear and the ability to manoeuvre easily and precisely throughout the operation. Mooring vessels designed for the work described are easily identifiable by the array of protective guards fitted to prevent mooring ropes becoming entangled with the mast, radar, wheelhouse and other parts of the superstructure. Most have an open stern and bulwarks of reduced height to enable ropes and hoses to be brought on deck easily. The size of vessel varies enormously, depending on the location at which they are required to work and the other duties they may have to perform. A small mooring vessel of about 14–16 metres in length is common at many terminals, and would be employed

Oil Bonny *was built for OIL Ltd in 1993 to provide mooring and other services at a Nigerian oil terminal. From the yard of McTay Marine at Bromborough, she is a twin screw vessel of 2350 bhp with a bollard pull of 25 tons. Note the overhead protective rails and cut-way bulwarks at the stern.*

(McTay Marine)

mainly to handle ropes and act as a tender to transport personnel and stores. Larger vessels, of up to 30 metres in length, may well be employed to carry out a wider range of duties, including giving towage assistance to small ships and providing fire-fighting and anti-pollution services.

Tugs and the dredging industry

The dredging industry has traditionally been a regular user of tugs to support its operations in ports and rivers around the world. Depending on the type of dredging operation in progress, tugs may be employed to carry out any of the following duties: towing non-propelled (dumb) hopper barges, moving and attending dredgers, surveying, and raking. The tugs used are invariably owned by port authorities, dredging companies, or contractors specialising in providing tugs for this type of work. In the industry today conventional screw tugs of the barge type, or small standard tugs of about 15 metres in length, are often used. The latter are frequently employed because of their versatility; they are highly manoeuvrable, economical to operate, and usually have suitable accommodation to house modern surveying equipment. In many cases the same tug can also be quickly adapted to tow a rake or plough. A very new development is a purpose-built vessel intended to fulfil all or most of the services demanded by the dredging industry. Marketed in Holland under the name "Dredgehelper", it is a powerful twin-screw tug with a broad shallow hull, equipped to tow, lift and rake.

The towing methods used are not in any way unusual. Hopper barges vary in size considerably, as do the journeys to the dumping grounds. Barges with a carrying capacity of 1,000 tons or more are common, and in some instances the tug is required to make long voyages towing loaded craft out to sea to be discharged. On other occasions the journey may be to a pumping plant where the spoil will be pumped ashore for reclamation purposes. The tug may also be required to reposition the dredger, pumping plant and floating pipelines. This often entails re-laying the anchors used to keep the dredger in the correct position; winches on board are used to control its position by hauling on the anchor cables. The tugs selected for a particular dredging operation are chosen with all these factors in mind.

Anchor-handling for a dredger is little different in principle to the operations carried out at sea for much larger oil rigs. The smaller anchors used with dredging craft may weigh a tonne or so and the tug may be required to recover and re-lay them when necessary. In order to avoid fouling the tug's own propeller with the anchor cable or recovery wire, the anchor may be hauled and secured near the tug's bow while running it to a new position.

Sophisticated electronic surveying equipment is increasingly employed by major dredging companies to enable accurate depth soundings to be carried out prior to, during and after dredging operations. This work is important to ensure that the correct depths have been achieved and the required amount of spoil removed. This equipment is often installed in one of the supporting tugs and may comprise depth-sounding equipment, coupled to an electronic charting system, to enable an accurate picture of the sea or river bed to be displayed on VDUs and recorded in the form of a printed chart.

Herman Senior *is equipped by her owners J L van Dodewaarrd of Zwijndrect, Holland, with a towed plough and extensive survey equipment to provide dredging support services in Europe. The vessel is 15.85 metres in length and has a Caterpillar main engine of 575 bhp to drive a single screw in a fixed Kort nozzle.* (Author)

An operation that is carried out by dredging tugs throughout Europe and elsewhere is "raking" or "ploughing". These terms refer to a very old process that has experienced something of a revival in recent years due to changes in modern dredging methods. To carry out the work a tug is used to tow a specially constructed steel rake along the sea or river bed to move unwanted mud or silt from around berths, moorings and in shipping channels. Often the tug works in conjunction with a self-propelled suction dredger and moves the spoil away from shallow areas and jetties to a point where the dredger can manoeuvre easily to pick it up for dumping at sea. This is a much cheaper method of keeping harbours cleared to the correct depth than employing more specialised dredgers. In order to carry out this work the tug requires a small winch and some form of "A" frame on the after deck to raise and lower the rake, which is usually towed by means of two chains or wires secured amidships, one on either side of the tug.

The use of tugs in civil engineering
The marine civil engineering industry is involved in construction projects such as bridges, tunnels, new port installations and, increasingly, the redevelopment of old dock systems throughout the world. Perhaps a less obvious aspect of the work is the continual improvement of sea defences and beaches, and the reclamation of new areas from the sea. As with the dredging industry, which is also heavily involved in some of this work, the use of tugs is almost unavoidable. Much of the work to be done, such as pile-driving, excavation and the installation of concrete and steel structures, can only be done using floating

plant and equipment. Cranes, piling barges, work platforms and barges for the transportation of materials all require assistance from tugs, and the great majority of these tasks are undertaken by vessels in the small tug category. Small, powerful twin-screw tugs and tug/workboats have proved ideal for such tasks. Much of the work, particularly with respect to sea defences, requires craft with sufficient power to handle unwieldy barges or pieces of floating plant, but with a draught shallow enough to work close inshore without constant risk of damage. The work of tugs and other vessels engaged on civil engineering projects is arduous. Working close alongside other vessels and pieces of floating plant for long periods of time, sometimes in a moderate swell, demands tugs of sturdy construction with carefully designed fendering.

Another group of vessels that have found a place with this industry are former ship-handling tugs that have been superseded in their original employment by newer "state of the art" vessels. These are often suitable to provide support on site, yet powerful enough to tow equipment on short coastal voyages from one project location to another. Also gaining in popularity, as previously mentioned, is the multi-purpose work vessel. The "multi-cat" has proved to be a very useful vessel to the civil engineer due to its shallow draught, ability to tow and generous deck space. Such a vessel is well suited to support pipe-laying, lifting, piling and diving

A new generation of towing and support vessels is marketed by Damen Marine Services of Hardinxveld as the "Dredgehelpers". DH Bravo was built in 1993, a vessel of 23.3 metres in length she has twin Cummins main engines producing 1160 bhp and giving a bollard pull of 17.4 tons. Note the large working deck and powerful hydraulic crane.   *(Damen Marine Services)*

operations. Most vessels of this type have a large portion of the hull divided into tanks for diesel fuel and fresh water, and are usually fitted with suitable transfer equipment to enable them to supply other vessels or plant.

Fish dock tugs

In the early days of towage, the fishing industry made good use of tugs to assist sailing vessels into port. A small number of tugs are still employed by the industry throughout the world, but in a quite different way. Once trawlers arrive in port after a lengthy voyage they are normally berthed to unload and the crews paid off. The vessel may then be required to move several times, to be repaired, refuelled and prepared for the next trip. Without a crew, she is regarded a "dead ship" and generally moved around the harbour by a tug. The tugs engaged in this work are generally small single-screw diesel vessels of about 300–500 bhp. Most of the towing is done with the tug fastened alongside her charge, which requires no crew on the fishing vessel to steer or handle lines. A tug with a sturdy hull and good fendering is required; she must be a "handy" vessel, sufficiently manoeuvrable to work in the frequently congested confines of a fish dock. In some parts of the world, where substantial fishing fleets are based, a larger tug may be employed to provide support for fishing vessels at sea. Such a vessel is used to tow home trawlers with machinery defects, transfer fuel and stores and provide similar services.

The 792 bhp twin screw tug ETA *spends much of her time in the port of Lowestoft assisting trawlers in the fish docks.* ETA *is a twin screw tug built in 1965 and owned by the Colne Shipping Company Ltd.* (*Author*)

Tugs used at fish farms

Small tugs are sometimes utilised by the operators of fish farms, particularly those situated at coastal sites and inland lochs. The tug or vessel of the tug/workboat type is a convenient vessel to tow the various items of equipment involved in the construction and maintenance of breeding cages and the supporting barges and pontoons. In this application the tug becomes a floating base, and one of the main requirements is to have adequate space on deck were work can be carried out. A small crane is often fitted and purpose-built vessels are usually equipped with push knees to assist with manoeuvring pontoons and cages.

Tugs in the timber business

In Canada, North America, Scandinavia and other areas where forestry is a thriving industry, timber is still transported by water in one form or another. Tugs are often involved in the process of getting tree trunks from riverside sites to sawmills using the waterways. Very small tugs are used to marshall these large logs at either end of the journey and in some cases assist in the construction of rafts made up of large numbers of logs. The vessels engaged in this work are very small, sturdy and agile craft well protected against damage to hull and propeller. The completed rafts of logs are in turn taken in tow to a sawmill for sorting and processing.

Alternatively, logs may be transported on special barges equipped for rapid loading and unloading. Where timber is to be pulped for the manufacture of paper or used in other wood-based products it may be reduced to wood chips at a plant near the forestry site. The chips are then transported in huge high-sided barges to the paper mills or factories. A variety of tugs are used for handling timber rafts and the barges mentioned, the main requirements being a suitably shallow draught to enable the tug to operate safely in shallow water, and sufficient power and manoeuvrability to move and control the tow in what may be difficult tidal conditions.

Wood chips are transported in and around British Columbia in very large barges. The picture shows a typical barge of over 1200 tons and a little twin screw tug Petro Master, *from the Rivtow fleet in Vancouver. Many very small tugs of between 13-15 metres in length and some 500–800 bhp operate in the area's timber trades.* (David Preston)

CHAPTER 6

Ship-handling and coastal tugs

Ship-handling tugs remain the most important category of vessel as far as development and evolution are concerned. A huge amount of effort continues to be expended in the development of tugs employed in the routine safe handling of ships, and the need for ship-handling tugs, in considerable numbers, will continue to exist in the foreseeable future. There are certain types of ship that will always require the assistance of tugs and, likewise, port areas that will remain accessible to ships only if towage can be provided. In very recent years these routine ship-handling services have been extended in many ports to include escort and emergency response duties. These additional duties involve the use of tugs to accompany very large ships, usually with volatile or otherwise hazardous cargoes, to and from locations well outside port limits. The tugs employed for this work are frequently purpose-built and often equipped to provide emergency anti-pollution measures should a serious accident occur. Escort tugs and their equipment are described in Chapter 7, but the ship-handling aspects of their work are covered later in this chapter.

Tug owners in the ship-handling business exist to provide the services mentioned above, but remain under constant pressure to do so at a reasonable cost, while facing increasing demands for power, performance and sophisticated equipment; commercial pressures continue to have a profound effect on tug design and operation. Tug owners now have a wide choice of hull and propulsion technology available to help them meet the demands of their clients effectively and, hopefully, economically. This chapter attempts to show how those choices are being exercised and give some idea of what ship-handling entails. Coastal tugs involved in the towage of ships, barges and other floating plant have been included in the same category as ship-handling vessels because the two types are so often fully interchangeable.

The tug owners

The ownership of ship-handling tugs varies, as it always has, with the global location and the needs of the individual port. In the major ports of the Western world tug fleets continue to get smaller, and the influence of major tug-owning groups appears to be increasing. Large groups of companies, controlling fleets in several locations at home and abroad, have become commonplace, being established throughout Britain, Europe, Australasia, the United States of America and the Far

On her arrival at Southampton the liner Queen Elizabeth II *is being swung through 180 degrees prior to berthing with the assistance of four tractor tugs.* Hamtun *and* Sir Bevios *from Red Funnel are vessels of Red Funnel Tugs and the* Flying Kestrel *and* Flying Osprey *from Howard Smith, all have a bollard pull of 35 tons. Two tugs are towing the ship round, one is pushing and one holding it against the tide.* (Author)

East. There are groups of companies operating fleets totalling 50–60 vessels in all of these locations, and some international companies with twice that number. The fleets are usually split up and deployed in quite small numbers of anything from one to 20 tugs in various ports. In Britain, for example, two large groups provide towage services in a great many locations. Howard Smith Towage & Salvage is an Australian-owned company that operates tug fleets at Hull, Immingham, Grimsby, Liverpool, London, Sheerness, Swansea, Southampton, Felixstowe and Gibraltar. Cory Towage Ltd has tug fleets in Belfast, Bristol, Newport, Cardiff, Milford Haven, Middlesbrough, Newcastle, Greenock and Liverpool, with financial interests in a number of other tug fleets in Britain and overseas. This pattern is repeated with the Moran, Foss and Crowley companies in the USA, Progemar in France, Smit International in Holland, and a great many others worldwide.

A useful by-product of group ownership is additional flexibility. The ability to transfer tugs of various types from one location to another within the group ensures that vessels are properly utilised and that individual ports have the most suitable craft available. There are also benefits to be gained from the purchasing power of a large group and the collective experience of employees working in different operational environments.

The situation in the former Eastern bloc is rather more volatile. Several tug fleets that were previously operated under state control in various parts of Russia, Poland, the former East Germany and elsewhere have found operating in a commercial environment difficult. Many have failed to compete with outside competition and others have formed joint ventures with western towage concerns, to their mutual benefit.

Small independent operators in the ship-handling business suffer mixed fortunes, particularly in the major ports of the world. Many ports that once employed several tug companies are now rarely serviced by more than one or two operators. Major established towage companies in many locations now face fierce competition from smaller independent operators and foreign companies bidding for ship-handling contracts. This has resulted in substantial reductions in the rates charged for towage operations, a situation welcomed by the ship owner but increasing the pressure on tug owners to reduce crews and employ fewer vessels. Many specialist services, involving fire-fighting, tanker-handling and escorting for example, require huge capital investment in vessels and are beyond the means of many smaller independent operators.

The approach to towage by the major port authorities is mixed, and many prefer not to become involved with providing towage services using their own resources. In much smaller ports, what towage services are necessary may be provided by the harbour authority, a small local operator, or by one of the larger groups. It is sometimes considered economical to employ a tug from a neighbouring port, entailing a short coastal passage.

Abeille Risban and other tugs of the Les Abeille (Progemar) fleet at the company's base in Dunkerque. The vessel is a Damen type 2900 (azimuthing) tractor tug of 2880 bhp and 35 tons bollard pull built in 1988. Approximately half a dozen vessels are present in the port at any one time, with occasional changes taking place among the various Progemar fleets in northern France. (Author)

The British navy frigate HMS Richmond *is seen being towed into Portsmouth by the Voith Schneider tractor* Bustler. *One of nine similar tugs she was built in 1981 and is a vessel of 375 gross tons, 38.8 metres in length and 2640 bhp.* (*Author*)

Ship-handling at naval bases in most of the major countries has traditionally been done by fleets of tugs owned and operated by the navy concerned. In the past this has resulted in large tug fleets maintained almost exclusively for the purpose. As the numbers of warships of a size requiring tug assistance have declined, as part of the so-called "peace dividend", tug fleets have also been reduced, and in some cases towage work has been put into the hands of commercial operators in order to cut costs. The type of work done at naval establishments involves ship-handling of the kind described later and some coastal operation. Special provision is often made at naval bases where very large and awkward ships such as aircraft carriers or nuclear submarines are handled. Tugs may require modifications to enable them to work beneath the overhanging flight deck of aircraft carriers, or special fendering and equipment to work with submarines.

Coastal towage is frequently a supplementary activity for the tug owner whose principal business is the operation of ship-handling tugs; this can provide useful additional revenue and help to ensure that tugs are fully utilised. To this end, major fleets often include vessels suitably equipped for coastal and short sea voyages with ships, barges or contracting plant in tow. Such vessels are equally capable of providing assistance to disabled ships in need of towage in coastal areas, another activity that attracts the small owner or one-man business. Without the substantial overheads of the larger concerns, such firms may compete for a wide range of coastal towage jobs at very competitive rates. As with the smaller tugs mentioned earlier, the vessels used are often former ship-handling tugs that have become outmoded in their original employment.

Types of tug for ship-handling

All of the three basic categories of tug described in Chapter 1, conventional screw tugs, tractors and stern-drive vessels, are in use for ship-handling operations, and there continues to be extensive debate in the industry on the merits of each. The

Knighton is a single screw, Kort nozzle, tug of 2000 bhp with a bollard pull of 30 tons, built by Richards Shipbuilders Ltd in 1968. The 34.6 metre long tug is seen here working on a vehicle carrier with other tugs of the Howard Smith Towage & Salvage fleet in the Medway port of Sheerness. (Author)

major factors governing the type of vessel used include the operational environment and the size of ships to be handled, as well as building, manning and running costs. Limitations placed on hull size and construction may apply to all three types; the maximum size of many ship-handling vessels is governed by the size of a port's locks or entrances, as it is often desirable for tugs to occupy the same lock as the ship being assisted, or be small enough to pass along her side. These limitations may apply regardless of the tug type. A vessel operating in exposed locations, or involved in coastal work, may require a hull with a raised forecastle to improve her sea-keeping qualities and help to keep the decks where men have to work free of water. A good free-running speed is a common requirement for ship-handling tugs to enable them to move quickly between tasks and possibly escort ships in the seaward approaches to a port. Figures of 12–14 knots are the norm, regardless of propulsion system.

In numerical terms conventional screw tugs, employing open screw propellers, Kort nozzles, and other thrust-augmenting devices, remain the most common type of vessel in service worldwide. However, this time-honoured means of propulsion is quickly being replaced in many major fleets by vessels using the tractor or stern-drive concepts.

In Britain and Europe alternative propulsion systems are being chosen for the vast majority of new vessels of any size entering service. There is, however, a large population of vessels, built since the mid-1970s with conventional screw propulsion, continuing to give good service, and that will remain in use for some time to come.

The more recent vary in size from 25 to 40 metres in length and 150 gross tons, ranging in power from 1,000 to 3,500 bhp. At the larger end of the scale they have bollard pulls of up to 50 tonnes and are used for work with large ships, or engaged in a high proportion of sea-going operations. The real advantage of the deep-draught, Kort nozzle tug is its ability to produce a high bollard pull at moderate power settings. By modern standards its handling characteristics may be limited, but are quite adequate for the work that it does. Similar relatively large tugs, employed as part of a ship-handling fleet, are often equipped with suitable deck and navigational equipment to enable them to operate efficiently at sea. Towing winches, carrying towlines suitable for both harbour towage and sea work on separate drums, are fitted to enable them to change roles with a minimum of additional preparation.

An important feature of any tug intended to work ships is its ability to reposition itself quickly during the towing operation, in order to apply power in the required direction. In this respect the conventional screw tug is somewhat limited and can in fact be endangered by her charge. One of the most common hazards is the risk of being capsized by the towline if the ship makes an unscheduled movement when the tug has the towline over her beam while repositioning. This phenomenon is known as "girding" or "girting", and has been responsible for the loss of many tugs. Among the safety features used in modern conventional tugs to minimise the risk are righting arms on towing hooks and the use of gog ropes; these have been

Large twin screw oil terminal tugs are popular among operators in the Arabian Gulf. The Al Hawtah *is a vessel of 42 metres in length and 752 gross tons built in Britain in 1991 by Richard Dunston Ltd for the Saudi Arabian Oil Company. Two Caterpillar main engines produce 4732 bhp to drive two controllable pitch propellers, incorporated in a "Towmaster" propulsion system, to give a 54 tons bollard pull going ahead and 52 tons astern.* (Danny Lynch)

described in preceding chapters. The ability of a modern tractor or stern-drive vessel to reposition easily and safely is probably its most important advantage when compared with the conventional screw tug.

The USA is one country that has been very slow to move away from tug designs employing the conventional screw propeller. With the exception of a small number of towing companies, it is only in very recent years that stern-drive and tractor tug designs have been adopted to any great degree. The majority of modern conventional tugs employed in ship-handling are twin-screw vessels, often with fixed and sometimes steerable Kort nozzles. A common additional refinement is the installation of flanking rudders, fitted ahead of the propellers. The power ratings quoted for some of the most recent vessels are as high as 6,000 bhp. Although comparable in size to their European counterparts, the American tug is often of heavier construction; the ship-handling methods used in the USA demand much more contact with the ship and thus an increased risk of damage. Towing bollards are still in use in most fleets, fitted on the foredeck and aft, while towing winches are installed aft on the more powerful and versatile vessels. In the last few decades the towing gear on some types of American tug has been installed further forward than was common in the past, closely resembling European practice. This is usually the case in vessels intended to work extensively with a towrope over the stern, rather than close alongside the tow.

The tugs used for ship-handling in many American ports are very much multi-purpose vessels, employed in fleets engaged in both ship-handling and barge towing. Many of the barges are very large and the journeys, on rivers and coasts, very long. Barges are pushed or towed depending on the circumstances – the pushing of barges is dealt with in Chapter 9.

Many American tugs are equipped to handle ships and barges. Seen here in the colours of the Mobil Oil Corporation of New York is the Tahchee *a single screw vessel of 191 gross tons and 3000 bhp built in 1973.* *(Michael Vincent)*

No. 90 is one of a large fleet of Voith Schneider tractor tugs operated by the port authority of Antwerp almost exclusively within the huge enclosed dock system. Built in 1989 by K Damen of Hardinxveld, she is 28.6 metres in length and has twin propulsion units driven by main engines of 2900 bhp. (Author)

The tractor tug has become a very popular means of assisting ships, particularly in ports where there are enclosed docks or riverside berths requiring intricate manoeuvres in difficult tidal conditions. The first tractors, introduced with the Voith Schneider propulsion system, brought a new dimension to the work. Their ability to apply thrust in any direction and handle equally well when going astern offered many new possibilities. Operating with the towline secured right aft virtually eliminates the possibility of the tug being capsized by her tow, improving safety considerably. Use of the tractor concept has spread to ports throughout the world, and Voith Schneider tractor tugs for ship-handling of over 5,000 bhp with bollard pulls in excess of 50 tonnes are now common in Britain, Europe, the USA and elsewhere. Such vessels are now widely used at sea, particularly when awkward positioning operations are carried out with barges or floating structures. Recent emphasis on escort services for very large ships has resulted in the development of Voith tractor tugs of huge proportions, largely for use from ports on the Pacific north-west coast of America. These vessels are designed to make maximum use of their large underwater skeg in the indirect towing mode.

Tractors incorporating azimuthing propulsion units are favoured by some operators for ship-handling and occasionally coastal towing. This approach combines the higher bollard pulls possible with the azimuthing unit with the inherent advantages of the tractor concept. A factor governing the use of tractors of either type may well be their draught; although the overall draught may be no more

Owned by J. Johannsen & Sohn of Lubeck, Axel *is a tractor tug of 30 metres in length and 3360 bhp with a bollard pull of 42 tons. The vessel is equipped with twin Schottel azimuthing propulsion units and was built in 1990 by the Hitzler Shipyard.* (Schottel)

The stern drive tug John *is one of four 4000 bhp sister vessels built by Matsuura Tekko Zosen in Japan in 1991 for Roda Bolaget of Gothenburg. She is a tug of 342 gross tons and 32 metres in length with a bollard pull of 53 tons. Note the two large towing winches on the fore deck. In the picture she bears the name* Portunus *during a period on charter to Red Funnel Tugs of Southampton.* (Author)

Waglan *and* Tai Tam *are identical stern drive tugs built in 1987 by Imamura Shipbuilding Co. of Japan for the Hong Kong Salvage & Towage Co. Ltd. Compact vessels of 22.6 metres and 181 gross tons, they have main engines of 2600 bhp and bollard pull of 32 tons.* *(Hong Kong S & T)*

than a deep screw tug, the position of the propulsion units protruding from the hull bottom plating makes them particularly vulnerable. In spite of nozzle or guard plates, the propellers of both types can be subject to damage if the tug is grounded. An objection raised by some owners is the additional complexity and cost of supporting this type of vessel during dry docking or hauling out on to a slipway.

A high proportion of new tugs entering service with ship-handling fleets is of the azimuthing stern-drive type. As we have seen, the basic design was first conceived in the Far East, but the concept has spread rapidly in the last decade or so to fleets in most parts of the world. A powerful propulsion system, sturdy hull, very basic towing gear, a central sophisticated control station, and accommodation for a small crew is the basic specification for many new tugs. Britain and Europe were slower to adopt the concept, as were operators in North America and Canada, a situation that is rapidly being reversed.

The stern-drive ship-handling vessel is always, by its nature, a twin-screw tug. Close-quarters towing is invariably carried out using towing gear or a winch located on the foredeck and towing astern. Operating in this way the tug is remarkably agile and can reposition, or move in to push with its fendered bow, very quickly, and the risk of girding is virtually nil. The bollard pull ahead or astern is almost identical in most vessels. Coastal work or operations requiring a much longer towline are carried out from the stern, much the same as with a conventional screw tug.

Ship-handling operations

Before attempting to show how the various types of modern tug are used, a few words on the basic purpose of the ship-handling tug may be useful. Tugs are employed to assist ships that, due to their size or design, are not capable of manoeuvring safely under their own power in the confined waters they may have to visit at either end of a voyage. The circumstances can vary from the use of a single relatively unsophisticated harbour tug assisting a medium-sized ship to its berth in a small port, to a complicated operation involving several powerful tugs working with a modern tanker of several hundred thousand tons.

The need for tugs

The need for tug assistance is determined by a multitude of factors: the size of the ship in relation to the area it is to enter, the need to negotiate locks, pass through bridges, or perform other complex manoeuvres to berth or unberth are all common reasons for employing some form of tug assistance. Difficult tidal conditions or high winds can impose severe limits on the handling of a ship in a confined waterway, and many small or medium-sized ships require assistance only when weather conditions are very poor. For example, large modern car and passenger ferries are well-equipped ships designed to handle well in all but the very worst weather conditions, but such vessels have very large superstructures that make them extremely susceptible to the effects of the wind in very bad conditions. A high wind, directly on her beam, may prevent any similar ship berthing or leaving safely without the assistance of a tug.

Larger ships have additional problems, related to the sheer bulk and enormous amount of kinetic energy inherent in their mass. A large ship, moving only very slowly, has sufficient stored energy to do a vast amount of damage should it collide with another object or even make contact with a jetty too heavily. It is the duty of the

Three tugs operated by Hunter Towage Services are shown handling the bulk carrier Iron Shortland, *a ship of 107,140 tons dw, at Newcastle NSW, Australia. Named* Carrington, Mayfield *and* Wickham *they are large Voith Schneider tractors of 37 metres in length, 496 gross tons and 4800 bhp with a 50 ton bollard pull. They were built in Europe and delivered in 1994.* *(Hunter Towage Services)*

attendant tugs to take charge of such ships, slow them down, move them on to their berth and stop any forward or sideways movement at exactly the right moment to prevent damage. The ship may need to be turned ("swung" in towage terms) in order to present the correct side to the berth for loading or discharge. Dock systems are often entered through locks and once inside can be congested, with narrow passages between the various basins. Tugs may be required to carry out these operations in a variety of tidal conditions, which alone can pose serious problems for large, unwieldy vessels.

Whether or not a ship requires the assistance of tugs is often an automatic decision. Many ports have bylaws that lay down strict rules governing pilotage and towage, and these generally place limits on the size and type of ship that can navigate in the area without tugs. Rules laid down by the ship's owners, insurance underwriters or wharf operators can also demand the assistance of tugs for certain vessels and circumstances, and these rules frequently give precise instructions on the number, type and power of the tugs to be used. When a very large ship enters port, decisions regarding her movements, pilotage and towage are usually made well in advance, leaving little to chance.

Computer simulation

Facilities now exist to determine by computer simulation the way that ship-handling operations are to be conducted. This is usually undertaken only when a major new towage situation arises; for example, where new berths are being commissioned for very large ships; a different type of ship is to use a facility; or drastic changes are to be made to the tug fleet. Computer programmes used for the work simulate local geography, tide and wind conditions, a ship's handling characteristics and the operational characteristics of the tugs employed. During a simulated ship-handling operation the positions of the tugs and their towing connections can be determined, and the heading of each tug and the power it exerts can be changed at will – in exactly the same way as an actual towage operation. The main difference is that the ship on the computer screen cannot be damaged or run aground causing expensive damage. From the information derived, decisions can be made regarding the number, position and power of all the assisting tugs and the optimum methods of carrying out a particular manoeuvre.

The role of the pilot

The role of the pilot is an important one. Pilotage arrangements differ from country to country, but in all cases the pilot is an individual with specific local knowledge of the port, its tides, and the effects of weather on the movement of ships. In most ports the use of a pilot is mandatory for ships above a certain size. Throughout Britain and Europe pilots are supplied either by the port authority or by a pilotage organisation, and join ships entering or leaving the area to advise the ship's master on the safe navigation of his vessel. Similar systems operate in many other parts of the world; in the USA the pilot may well be a senior tug master, from one of the tugs assisting the ship, put on board to take charge of the operation. It is necessary for a pilot, using tugs in a modern port, to have a sound knowledge of the capability of the various tugs he is using, and an appreciation of the advantages and disadvantages of the various propulsion systems. During a ship-handling operation the pilot is in charge of any tugs used and communicates his orders directly to the tug masters by VHF radio; the use of whistle signals between tug and ship has been superseded by radio in most ports, except in emergencies.

Basic ship-handling manoeuvres

A tug master will say that every task is different – different weather and tidal conditions, different ships each with their own characteristics, and perhaps different pilots. All of the foregoing factors play a part in towage operations in almost any port in the world.

The next few paragraphs are not intended as definitive examples, but simply to illustrate some of the very basic manoeuvres that tugs are regularly expected to perform while ship-handling. They also give some indication of how these operations vary with the type of tug. The descriptions do not take into account the possible effects of wind and tide, which can transform the simplest operation into a nightmare. It is also worth considering that these operations are carried out daily by tug crews, working not only in fine daylight conditions but also at night and throughout the winter months. The work has to continue in the dark, with the tug rolling and with decks and ropes covered with ice or snow. Even in the best-equipped tug, personnel are still required to work on deck to handle the towline and make the initial connection between ship and tug.

Picking up the tow

One of the most interesting operations to watch, and one requiring a great deal of skill from both tug master and crew, is "picking up a tow" while the ship is under

The Shalder *is shown manoeuvring close under the bow of the tanker* Tatina *to make a towing connection. Only a few metres separate the two vessels.* Shalder *is a Voith Schneider tractor of 4000 bhp, built for the Shetland Towage Company by Ferguson Shipbuilders in 1983.* (Shetland Towage)

Sun Anglia is travelling stern first in the wake of a fast moving container ship to put her towline aboard in readiness to help slow or steer the vessel. The tug is a 3400 bhp Voith Schneider tractor from the fleet of Howard Smith Towage & Salvage at Gravesend and seen here in the livery of predecessors Alexandra Towing. (Author)

way. When a ship enters port, or approaches a berth, it will often try to maintain sufficient speed to enable it to steer effectively until the tugs have their towlines connected; the tugs may have to approach it and connect towlines with the ship moving as fast as 5–6 knots. This can be a hazardous operation, particularly for the tug selected to take charge of the ship's bow – the "head tug". The flow of water around the hull of a large moving ship produces a phenomenon known as "interaction"; a situation can arise in which the tug passes into a low-pressure area adjacent to the ship's bow, causing loss of control. This can result in a collision or in the tug being run down by the ship.

In order for a towline to be passed, the tug will manoeuvre within a very few metres of the ship's bow. A conventional screw tug is the most vulnerable during this operation; tractors or stern-drive tugs are able to control the thrust from their propulsion units to combat any risk of collision, while some stern-drive vessels are able to manoeuvre astern at speed and may use this method to position the bow of the tug in readiness to connect a towline from the forward winch.

Once the tug is in position, a heaving line is thrown down from the ship to the waiting tug crew. The heaving line is tied to the end of a light "messenger" rope, which is then used to haul the towline aboard the ship. In some ports a rope from the ship may be used, but with the special nature of modern towropes and the use of towing winches it is now more common for the tug's ropes to be used. With the towline secured, the tug can move into a towing position.

For tugs at the stern or alongside the ship, picking up the tow is slightly easier, although a stern tug may be affected by wash from the ship's propeller. A conventional screw tug or stern-drive vessel will approach from astern and put her bow in a position very close to the ship's stern prior to receiving a heaving line. Tractor tugs in the same situation usually approach in the same manner but travelling stern-first. Once the towing connection is made, a tractor or stern-drive tug will simply drop back into a towing position paying out the towline to a convenient length. A conventional screw tug will make a towing connection on her winch or hook aft and move out to one side, continuing to go ahead parallel to the ship until the speed of the ship is reduced sufficiently to enable her to safely turn through 180 degrees and take up a towing position.

American-style conventional tugs move in alongside the ship and make a connection with short towropes from the bow of each tug. Tugs that are to remain alongside for the whole operation, parallel to the ship, may also be secured by a rope aft.

Slowing a ship down
Prior to positioning the ship for berthing it will be slowed down and stopped in the correct position. Using European methods, the stern tug will be positioned to tow astern and slow the ship, leaving the head tug to control the ship's direction. Under these circumstances the tug or tractor is towed along, stern-first, by the ship, applying power when necessary and acting rather like a rudder. A stern-drive tug will operate in much the same manner, but will be connected from its bow and apply power by going astern. Alternatively, the pilot will rely on the ship's own power to stop the ship and use the tugs to assist in steering.

The 162,000 tons dw bulk carrier Lowland Trassey *is being swung in Belfast by tugs of the Cory Towage fleet. The tugs (left to right)* Thunderer, Coleraine, Cultra *and* Clandeboye *have a combined maximum bollard pull of some 120 tons.* *(Alan Geddes)*

American tugs apply power astern, selectively, at the pilot's instruction to keep the ship on course. If required, a selected tug can reposition easily and move ahead if required.

When a tug is operating in the escort role the process of slowing a ship down can have entirely different implications due to the probable size of the ship and momentum involved. Escort duties are described in Chapter 7.

"Swinging" a ship

"Swinging", or turning, a ship is a basic manoeuvre used to turn the vessel through 180 degrees, into a tide prior to berthing or to ensure that the correct side of the ship is in contact with the berth for loading or unloading purposes. A partial "swing" may be used to

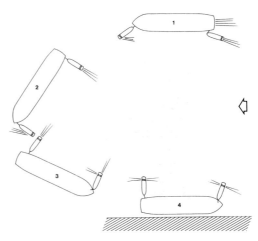

A swinging and berthing operation with modern stern drive tugs is normally undertaken with each tug connected by a towline from it's bow. The arrow indicates the direction of the tide, the direction of thrust from each of the tug's propulsion units is also shown.

turn a ship into a lock or dock entrance. If the ship is to be turned to starboard, using European practice, the head tug will move round to tow at 90 degrees to the ship's starboard side. A stern tug will position herself similarly port and the ship, which will be turned bodily under the direction of the pilot. If other tugs are involved with berthing the ship they may be called in to push on bow or stern to assist or control the swing. In some cases more than one head tug will be used. If

The sequence of operations likely to be adopted by a pair of conventional screw tugs manoeuvring a ship into a lock or entrance from a tidal river. The arrove indicates the tidal flow.

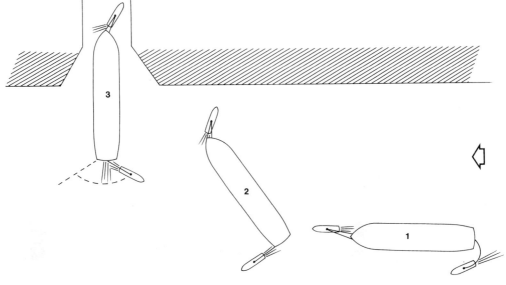

tractor tugs are used, repositioning to tow to port or starboard is a simple matter and can be achieved safely keeping control of the towline. Again, the stern-drive tug will perform in much the same way – towing astern or pushing on the ship's bow or stern.

If the ship is to be turned into a lock or entrance, the head tug is responsible for aligning the ship's bow with the opening. The stern tug then has the task of holding the stern in line, working to counteract any crosswind or tidal flow. Any additional tugs may be deployed along the ship's side to push or guide the vessel, reducing the contact with the lock walls.

American tugs undertaking a "swinging" operation will tow astern to port or starboard as appropriate, or push on the ship's bow and stern. If tugs are positioned on either side of the ship, secured bow and stern, one will put her engines ahead and the other astern, creating a powerful turning moment. Moving the ship into an

A ship is being held in position against the wharf by the two compact stern drive tugs Seaspan Hawk *and* Seaspan Falcon. *Built in 1993 for Seaspan International Ltd of Vancouver, they are 24.4 metres in length and propelled by Detroit main engines of 3000 bhp and Niigata "Z" drive units. The tugs have a bollard pull of 40 tons and a two man crew.* (Seaspan)

entrance is done in much the same way, pushing or backing away on the short towropes.

Berthing a ship alongside

Any manoeuvres carried out with a ship prior to her arrival at a wharf or jetty are usually designed to end with the vessel positioned conveniently near the berth; often this results in the ship being positioned parallel to the berth but some distance away. In European practice head and stern tugs will tow towards the berth, moving the ship sideways. By co-ordinating the work of the tugs at each end the pilot can also ensure that the ship is correctly positioned longitudinally. Additional tugs may be employed to push on the vessel's side. Once the ship is close enough for mooring ropes to be passed, one or other of the tugs may be released, leaving the other to hold the ship in position against any tide or wind. The free tug may then be used to push on the ship's side to relieve the pressure on mooring lines until all the ropes are secure.

The use of tractors or stern-drive tugs in the foregoing operation simplifies matters considerably. A tractor will tow the ship into position in much the same way, but once the first mooring lines are passed she can adjust the length of her towline and move in quickly to push with her stern, without the need to disconnect. Stern-drive tugs, working from a bow winch, operate in the same fashion. American tugs carrying out the same operation remain connected by the bow and move round to push at 90 degrees to the ship. If some adjustment is required to the longitudinal

Two conventional screw tugs, Eileen McAllister *and* McAllister Sisters, *manoeuvre the tanker* Hawaiian Express *(29,998 tons dw) in New York. Each is connected by a short rope to the ship enabling them to push or back away as required.* *(Michael Vincent)*

Two Japanese built stern drive tugs Lady Brenda *and* Lady Morag, *from the Howard Smith fleet, tow a car carrier away from its berth at Sheerness. Both tugs are towing from their forward winches in a true push/pull mode of operation.* (Author)

position, one or more tugs will move parallel to the ship and apply power in the necessary direction.

Although the practice of tugs pushing on a ship's side is an inherent part of ship-handling operations, it is undertaken with some caution as a powerful tug is capable of causing serious damage to the side plating of some ships. In a heavy swell it may be particularly difficult to keep the tug properly positioned on the ship's side. Some modern ships have marks painted along their sides indicating the correct "pressure points" where assisting tugs may push without causing damage.

Assisting a ship away from a berth
For relatively large ships, the procedure for leaving a berth is very much the reverse of that used for berthing. Depending on the size of the ship, the weather conditions and the need for any subsequent manoeuvres, a little less assistance may be needed. Ships are often berthed "head down", heading downstream or towards the port entrance, having been "swung" on arrival, simplifying matters when they depart. The head and stern tugs are connected as before and are positioned initially to tow the ship sideways off the berth. An additional tug may be used to push on the ship's side, holding it in position while the mooring ropes are released. Once the ship is ready to leave and has been moved off the berth sufficiently, the head tug will

impart some forward motion, towing the ship in the direction she is to head. Generally the head tug will remain connected until any other tugs have been released and the pilot is assured that the ship's steering and propulsion systems are working correctly.

American-style tugs will also use the reverse procedure to that of berthing. The tugs will each be connected with a rope from the bow and tow out stern-first. With very large ships tugs may also move in to push on the bow and stern, on the shore side of the ship, once the mooring ropes have be released. Because American tugs operate in such close proximity to their charges, they frequently sustain superficial damage. For instance, manoeuvring beneath the overhanging bow and stern areas of large ships sometimes results in damaged masts, wheelhouses and hand-rails.

In high winds, even ships that do not normally need assistance from tugs may have difficulty leaving a berth without help. A ship can be held firmly against the quay by a stiff breeze, and the assistance of just one tug may be all that is required to tow the vessel's bow or stern away from the berth and perhaps impart some forward movement.

Indirect towing
In recent years considerable effort has been applied to developing "indirect towing" methods as a means of enabling a tug to exert dynamic forces on the towline

The top diagram shows a typical indirect towing position for a tractor tug when steering or slowing a ship. By using the thrust from it's propulsion units the tug is held at an oblique angle to the towline to increase resistance and act in much the same way as a very large rudder. The lower drawing shows a stern drive vessel operating in a similar way, towing from it's forward winch.

Tractor tug Tirrick *of Shetland Towage is acting as stern tug on a large tanker and being towed through the water by the ship. When necessary* Tirrick *adopts an indirect towing position to slow the ship and assist with steering.* *(Shetland)*

considerably in excess of its static bollard pull. As previously mentioned in Chapter 1, the masters of early steam and motor tugs, with very low bollard pull performance, often used the weight and bulk of their vessels to exert additional force to stop or turn a ship. This was done, with careful use of a gob rope, by turning the tug at an angle to the towline and using their power to control its position – producing an effect rather like a massive rudder or sea anchor. The term "indirect towing" is relatively new, but the principles involved can be traced back to those early methods.

Indirect towing is now used extensively to improve the performance of escort tugs working with very large ships, particularly ships under way requiring assistance to stop or be steered. Many will argue that the Voith Schneider tractor tug is inherently suited to the task due to its very large underwater skeg. When acting as stern tug, with a ship under way, the tractor is turned obliquely to the towline to produce an "otter-board" or "paravane" effect. The tug can be positioned to produce a steering force or braking effect of at least twice its normal bollard pull using this method. A tractor tug used extensively in this manner will be provided with an additional towing fairlead further aft than that normally used for ship-handling. The fairlead is positioned above the trailing edge of the underwater skeg to reduce steering forces when the tractor is being towed stern-first.

Indirect towing is a method also used by stern-drive tugs operating in the escort role. Much effort has gone into improving the effectiveness of such vessels in this role by modifying their underwater shape to increase resistance when operating at an oblique angle to the towline. Stern-drive tugs operating in this way normally tow from their forward winch and use their propulsion units to maintain position.

Retrieving the towline

The final action, once a towing operation is completed, is to retrieve the towline safely without fouling the propellers of the ship or the tug herself. Even when the ship is stationary there is need for caution. A conventional screw tug, operating with a towline aft, normally moves steadily away from the ship, allowing the towline to stream astern; Norman pins will often be erected at the after rail to ensure that the rope does not pass over the side and become drawn into the propeller. Tugs fitted with towing winches can retrieve their ropes quickly. Others may use some form of rope recovery technique, using a messenger rope and a capstan or some other means of getting the rope inboard with as little manual effort as possible. Caution is also required with tractors and stern-drive tugs, though these have the advantage of the propellers being located further away from the towing gear. The master is also able to manoeuvre easily in a manner that will reduce the danger of fouling the propulsion units.

Coastal towing

Coastal towing is a generic term often used to cover a wide range of operations. In Europe, voyages between neighbouring countries are often shorter than many coastal trips but encounter similar conditions to true deep-sea towing. Coastal towing around the continents of North and South America, Africa, Russia and southern Asia is quite a different matter, and can involve vast distances. In the context of this chapter coastal towing covers the tasks likely to be undertaken by ship-handling tugs or vessels of similar size and type.

There are regulations governing the towage of ships and other floating objects on coastal and intercontinental voyages, and these continue to become more stringent. Such regulations are laid down by the various transport ministries, classification societies, insurers, and, in some cases, coastguard authorities. Within the various rules are requirements governing the size and power of tugs, the types of towing gear used, minimum standards for safety equipment and often recommendations governing the conduct of voyages. Many tugs employed primarily for ship-handling are also designed to meet the conditions laid down, in terms of power, bollard pull, and equipment. Vessels operated by companies specialising in coastal towage have to conform as a matter of course and may meet higher standards for worldwide operation.

The tug and its equipment

Obviously, the size and power of the tug used for a particular towing operation is related to the nature of the vessel to be towed. As we have already seen, vessels in the smaller tug categories also make coastal voyages under certain circumstances. Tugs regularly involved in this type of work will range in power from 1,200 to 6,000 bhp and in size from 150 to 500 gross tons. Many vessels operating regularly on the

Towing Witch is a twin screw seagoing tug employed almost exclusively on coastal and short sea towage by the British company TSA Tugs Ltd. She was built in 1965 and is a vessel of 541 gross tons and 44 metres in length with a bollard pull of 42 tons. (*Author*)

coastal routes of the American continent may well be even larger and more powerful. Most of the tugs employed for coastal work will be single- or twin-screw conventional tugs with good sea-keeping characteristics.

A tug equipped for regular coastal work will be fitted with a suitable towing winch to enable the length of the towline to be adjusted with a minimum of effort. Such winches are usually of the drum type and may carry steel wire towlines of 600–1,000 metres in length. Longer towlines are needed for towing at sea than for harbour or ship-handling work. Tugs without a winch require a powerful capstan or some other aid to handle the towline, particularly at either end of the voyage.

The range of most tugs of a suitable size is likely to be adequate for coastal towing operations, but fuel consumption is heavily dependent on the type of tow and the weather conditions. A full outfit of radar, communications and electronic position-finding equipment is a requirement for coastal vessels under most national regulations. Also, sufficient capacity is needed to stow domestic stores, food, fresh water, spare ropes and other equipment to make the vessel relatively self-supporting for short periods.

The towing operation

In essence, a coastal or short sea towage operation is tackled in very much the same way as a full-scale ocean-going voyage; the basic principles are similar and many of the same considerations apply. The type of vessel to be towed may also be similar. A common task for the coastal tug is the small and medium-sized ship that requires assistance due to machinery damage. Similar unmanned vessels are frequently towed between ports for repair or to scrapyards for breaking, while large barges, dredgers, construction rigs and cranes are all vessels regularly towed between ports and marine construction sites. Barges used for the transport of construction materials, such as stone, steel piles and concrete structures, are often at sea constantly, towed by various contractors in different areas as the work dictates.

Some of the vessels requiring towage behave very badly under tow and can present many difficulties for the tug master and crew; with many such vessels the need to be towed was not a serious consideration in the original design. Awkward tows behave in various ways: some yaw from side to side, others sheer off to one side, and may even overtake the tug under certain conditions. The most dangerous and challenging for the tug master is one that behaves in a totally unpredictable manner. Ships are generally among the easier subjects for towing at sea, but even some of these can prove difficult.

Before leaving port a survey is carried out by a marine surveyor on behalf of the insurers, the classification society, or the relevant government agency. The specification for the tug will be checked, as well as the towing gear and the condition of the vessel to be towed. Some temporary preparation may be required in readiness for towing. On a small ship, windows and openings may be boarded up,

A redundant warship. Andromeda, *is being towed by the single screw harbour and coastal tug* Conor. *The chain bridle in the towing connection is clearly visible.* Conor *is a tug of 302 gross tons and 34 metres in length with a 3000 bhp Deutz main engine and a 43 ton bollard pull. She is owned by West Coast Towing (UK) Ltd.* (Author)

deck equipment lashed down and the rudder firmly secured in the amidships position. The propeller shaft may be disconnected to enable the propeller to rotate freely without causing drag, or firmly secured to prevent rotation and possible damage to machinery.

The towing gear will be rigged aboard the tow in a manner designed to reduce the possibility of the connection breaking due to wear or chafing. The towline is particularly vulnerable to damage where it passes through fairleads and is secured around bitts, so short lengths of chain may be used to make the towing connection at this point. A length of large-diameter nylon rope is often coupled into the towline as a "spring" to absorb some of the shock loads that occur during towing. An additional emergency towline may also be rigged and stowed on the towed vessel where it can be quickly retrieved should the main towline break. In an unmanned tow, provision is also made for the necessary lights to be rigged and working before the vessels leave harbour.

A tug leaving harbour with a tow may need the assistance of another tug to help control the tow until open water is reached. Alternatively, if the towed vessel is small but awkward the tug may be secured alongside, to give the tug master better control. The towline will be rigged in readiness and the vessel streamed astern when

The German tug Ems Pull *is a former ship-handling tug of 1700 bhp and 24 tons bollard pull, built in 1970. The single screw tug is towing a pontoon barge loaded with six liquid gas storage tanks.* (Author)

The coastal traffic around the seaboard of the America and Canada includes many tugs and barges with all kinds of cargo. The single screw tug Kincome, *is seen entering the port of Vancouver with a barge load of rail cars.* *(Paul Andow)*

there is sufficient "sea room". Once at sea the length of the towline may need adjustment; the length required will be determined mainly by the size of the tow and the weather conditions. The effects of towline length and other factors concerning towing at sea are explained in a later chapter on deep-sea tugs and towing. In a tug with a towing winch this is a minor matter, but for vessels without this facility, lengthening a towline and later shortening it to enter harbour can be a major task, involving the use of the capstan and gripping devices known as "stoppers". This is a time-consuming operation, requiring a high level of seamanship, in which the towline is paid out or hauled in in short stages.

While the tug is at sea with a tow, a constant watch is kept on the condition of the towing gear. Any points on the towline where it might become chafed and damaged, through contact with tow beams or other parts of the vessel, are protected. At night the towline, and if possible the vessel in tow, will be inspected using a searchlight. The crew will work to a sea-going watch system of four hours on duty and four off, but in coastal waters the tug master is unlikely to leave the wheelhouse for any length of time. Radar will be used to monitor the position of any other traffic in the vicinity of the tug or tow, and radio contact will be maintained with coastguards and other shore stations; in some areas regular contact with such stations is mandatory.

CHAPTER 7

Tugs for escort, pollution-control, fire-fighting, and ice-breaking duties

Over the years tugs have evolved to carry out many specialist duties in addition to their normal towage work, and among the best known of these are escorting, fire-fighting, pollution-control and ice-breaking. The towage industry is becoming increasingly involved in the protection of life and the environment from marine pollution and the hazards of fire at marine terminals. An important part of that protection is the provision of escort services to very large tankers and other ships carrying hazardous cargoes. The result of this involvement is a whole new generation of tugs that are emerging to deal with all aspects of escort, fire-protection and pollution control. A less emotive but continuing problem for northern ports is that of winter ice. For many decades an ice-breaking service has been provided by local tug fleets to keep shipping lanes open for as long as possible during the winter months.

Escort services
Following a number of serious oil tanker accidents in the past decade, some of which resulted in oil pollution of catastrophic proportions, there has been enormous public pressure to improve the safety of marine transportation and tanker operation in particular. One of the ways that oil companies and tanker operators reacted to this pressure was to implement the greater use of escorting tugs for large ships in coastal waters, the intention being to have a tug immediately to hand should a fully loaded tanker suffer a loss of power, steering, or other serious failure. The extent of this service varies considerably with geography and the client's perception of the potential risk, but several schemes are in being at oil terminals around the world and others are being considered. Such measures have been given particular prominence in North America where Federal law gives individual states and the coastguard wide powers in matters concerning pollution hazards.

A typical requirement is for ships of over 70,000 tons dead weight to be escorted for distances of anything between 2 and 25 miles, and sometimes further. If a propulsion or steering failure occurs aboard the tanker it is the task of the tug to stop or steer the ship effectively and control it until further assistance can be made available, or a safe anchorage achieved. To stop or steer the offending ship sounds simple enough in normal ship-handling terms, but the size and speed of the ship become critical factors in this scenario. A fully loaded tanker of perhaps 250,000

Silex is performing escort duty with the Hellespont Grand, *a tanker of 420,000 tons dw on route to the Esso oil terminal at Fawley. The tug has her towline connected to the stern of the tanker to provide immediate assistance in an emergency.* Silex *is a tanker handling and escort tug of 5386 bhp with 60 ton bollard pull operated by Solent Towage Ltd.* (Johannes Ostensjo)

tons approaching its destination may well be travelling at over 10 knots when she is met by the escort some miles from shore. In the approach channels the ship's master may be reluctant to reduce speed until absolutely necessary in order to retain a reasonable degree of steerage. Therefore the escort tug requires not only the power to render real assistance, but a good margin of speed.

For the tug operator, escorting raises a number of serious issues, mainly concerned with ensuring that such services can be provided effectively and economically. The ability of a single tug to perform the necessary duties is a key issue, particularly where long distances are involved. Many oil terminals are in remote locations with dedicated tug fleets on station to provide ship-handling assistance and often fire-fighting protection. The additional demand for a tug to escort ships over long distances to and from jetties can impose a serious burden on many such fleets. There are also serious legal implications for the tug operator regarding liability should an incident occur while an escort tug is in attendance – fortunately, this is a matter still to be tested at the time of writing.

The escort tug
The important issue of what type of tug can be effective in the escort role remains one of the most contentious aspects of the whole subject. In the past, most new demands placed on ship-handling tugs have been met with more powerful vessels or advanced propulsion technology to improve manoeuvrability and safety. Bollard pull is important, but may not necessarily be the deciding factor when working with a large ship at high speeds. Figures of between 55 and 90 tons bollard pull are often quoted, but some owners are ordering purpose-built escort tugs capable of much larger figures. The lower figure is one that can be met by an increasing number of modern ship-handling tugs, but the environment in which the escort vessel may have to operate and the distances involved may render them unsuitable. Much of the distance an escort will be required to cover may be at sea in areas with

Cramond is one of a pair of tugs built for BP Oil in 1993 for tanker handling and emergency response duties at the Hound Point terminal in Scotland. A stern drive vessel of 448 gross tons and 34.85 metres in length, she has main engines of 4800 bhp and a bollard pull of 60 tonnes. A good free running speed of 14 knots is typical of many escort tugs. (*Author*)

predominantly poor weather for much of the year. A substantial forecastle is therefore a prime requirement in most purpose-built vessels. Free running speed is also an important factor; the normal service speed of a ship-handling tug of 12–13 knots is regarded as marginal in some instances.

The towage industry remains divided as to the type of propulsion technology ideally suited to escort duties. A large stern-drive tug of some 35–45 metres in length, with a high forecastle and a bollard pull of between 60 and 95 tonnes is the choice of many operators. Such vessels are of course equipped to tow over the bow and will have a hull form designed to be effective in the indirect towing mode. Other operators have put their faith in large, powerful Voith Schneider tractor tugs optimised to perform well when operating stern-first. A tractor for use in escort work is likely to have a stern giving more freeboard than usual and a towing fairlead positioned very close to the stern. On the north-west coast of America at Puget Sound, Voith tractors of very large proportions are employed to escort tankers over long distances in a very sensitive area. The tugs concerned are 47 metres in length, with a massive draught of over 6 metres, powered by main engines of almost 8,000 brake horsepower. It is argued that tractor tugs of this type and many smaller ones in use elsewhere can exert towline pulls far exceeding their bollard pull when towing in the indirect mode, due to the very large surface area of the underwater skeg.

An escort tug is sometimes referred to as an "intervention vessel" or an "emergency response vessel". In many cases these terms refer to vessels that are employed largely to provide safety-orientated services such as escorting, fire-fighting and pollution-control work, and may have little involvement in the actual berthing of ships. More commonly the escort tug is equipped to carry out those functions in addition to her normal ship-handling duties. To that end a "state of the art" escort tug will be fitted for fire-fighting to a high standard, and often carry the necessary equipment to deploy protective booms and carry out oil retrieval. All of these subjects are dealt with later in this chapter.

Escort operations

The duties of the escort tug, with regard to incoming ships, start at a rendezvous point at sea, often at the seaward limit of the port concerned. In most cases, on meeting the tanker a towing connection will be established, with the tug's towline

The Voith Schneider tug Tystie *is one of a pair built for escort, tanker-handling and emergency response duties at Sullom Voe, Shetland, where weather conditions can be difficult and unpredictable. The 5516 bhp vessel is 38.6 metres in length and 797 gross tons.* Tystie *is fitted with two towing winches, one on deck for normal use and one housed within the superstructure for use at sea.* (Author)

being made fast at a central point on the stern of the ship. This is regarded as an "active" escort, where the tug can respond immediately to assist the ship to steer or stop if required. An alternative arrangement would be to have the tug accompany the ship at close quarters without making a connection until much later in the operation; this would involve a time delay of some minutes should the ship require help in an emergency.

Approaching the ship to make a towing connection presents no great problem for either the stern-drive or purpose-built tractor tug, in spite of the ship's speed, which may well be in excess of 10 knots. The stern-drive tug will be positioned with her bow close to the stern of the ship and pass the towline from the forward winch in the normal way, an operation that can be carried out relatively safely at sea. The tractor will turn stern-first and make a connection in the same manner from the winch, passing the towline through the aftermost towing fairlead.

Once a towing connection is made the tug will maintain a position astern of the ship, usually keeping the towline slack. In this way the ship is not inhibited in any way by towing the tug, and wear on the towline is considerably reduced. If the ship suffers a serious malfunction, the prime task of the escort tug is to assist the vessel to achieve a safe anchorage or maintain a course within the designated shipping channels. It is generally considered most likely that the tug will be required to slow and steer the ship rather than attempt to bring it immediately to a halt. In either case considerable skill and effort is needed to provide the necessary assistance to a very large ship of up to 500,000 tons.

The tractor tug Redbridge *is connected as escort to the tanker Wapello in Southampton Water. In this role her towline passes through a special fairlead in her after bulwarks. The 4104 bhp tug has a bollard pull of 45 tonnes and is optimised to run stern first in tis situation.* (Author)

The stern-drive tug in this situation may initially apply full power astern, with the azimuthing propulsion units directing thrust forward, to slow the ship. Alternatively, when assisting a ship at very high speed, a method known as the "transverse arrest" mode may be used. In this mode the propulsion units are turned outboard to their normal neutral position but with full power applied, a method claimed to produce massive drag and very high towline forces. A tractor tug will likewise apply full power astern, but both types of tug will quickly resort to indirect towing methods (see Chapter 6) in order to apply sufficient force to the towline to slow or steer the ship successfully.

In most locations the same large ships are also escorted on the outward-bound journey from the berth to sea. The extent of escort services in other areas often depends on whether the ships are fully loaded or in a light condition, the former being accompanied by a tug at all times.

Fire-fighting

The enormous traffic in ships carrying oil, petrochemicals and dangerous liquefied gases has resulted in comprehensive fire-protection measures being put into place in ports and at specialist loading and unloading terminals, and these measures usually include the provision of specially equipped fire-fighting vessels. In the vast majority of ports and terminals this duty has been taken on by the local tug fleet; where tugs are already on station to provide ship-handling services, often on a 24-hour basis, it has made good economic sense to install comprehensive fire-fighting equipment aboard some or all of the vessels involved. The cost of providing continuous fire-fighting protection is generally met by special contracts placed with the tug owners by the oil terminal operators or port authorities. Additional finance may also come from local or central government sources.

Thankfully, most fire fighting tugs rarely use their equipment in a serious emergency. Here the Ribut *of Bureau Wysmuller fights a major fire aboard a tanker in the Arabian Gulf.* (*Wysmuller*)

An important factor in the operation of fire tugs is the provision of specialist fire-fighting expertise, and here the approach varies. Tug crews often receive special training in fire-fighting in order to achieve their vocational qualifications, while a common method of providing additional expertise is to take on board trained fire-fighters when a full-scale emergency occurs. This procedure is used extensively in Britain, where local fire brigade personnel regularly go aboard fire-fighting tugs to become familiar with the equipment and to train in conjunction with the tug crews.

The fire tug
Fortunately, fire fighting is very much a secondary duty – the vast majority of fire tugs have never been called upon to combat a serious fire. Therefore when vessels are built and equipped, towage requirements remain paramount. The only

exceptions to this are the very few full-time fire-fighting vessels operated by port authorities. These are frequently based on tug designs but would normally undertake towing only in an extreme emergency.

There are a number of basic features the tug must possess to be suitable for use as a fire-fighting vessel, the most important being adequate power to operate the fire pumps. High-performance fire pumps in modern ship-handling tugs are usually driven by the main engines, often with one pump on each main engine in a twin-engined vessel. Using this method the engine or propulsion controls are designed to ensure that sufficient power remains available to manoeuvre the tug while the pumps are in operation. Alternatively, pumps driven by separate auxiliary diesel engines may be installed. Ideally these are located in the engine room, for protection and stability reasons, but they are occasionally located in the superstructure or on deck. The power needed and the size of the fire pumps varies with the number of monitors fitted and their capacity, but figures in excess of 600 bhp are not uncommon.

Manoeuvrability is also an important consideration. In the event of a fire – aboard a ship or at a shore installation – the tug must be accurately positioned to enable the fire-fighters to do their work. A less obvious need is the ability to manoeuvre precisely and counteract the thrust generated by the monitors. Very powerful monitors produce considerable thrust, and can make controlling the

The fire monitors aboard Sayyaf *are capable of delivering 1200 tonnes of water per hour in jets reaching 120 metres. Foam compound may also be used and the tug may be protected by a water dowsing system.* Sayyaf *is a twin screw tanker handling tug of 680 gross tons and 40 metres in length with a bollard pull of 57 tonnes – built for the Abu Dhabi Oil Producers Operating Company in 1994.* (McTay Marine)

vessel's position extremely difficult. For this reason highly manoeuvrable tractor tugs and stern-drive vessels make ideal fire tugs. During a fire-fighting operation there may be circumstances when the jets of water or foam from the monitors can only be directed satisfactorily by manoeuvring the entire vessel. If the monitors have no remote controls, once they have been adjusted it may be too hot for the crew to remain on deck to control them. Under these conditions it is essential that the tug handles well with the fire monitors in operation.

Fire-fighting equipment
Fire-fighting monitors have already been mentioned a number of times, including a brief description in Chapter 4. In the modern fire tug at least two high-capacity monitors will be installed, of a type capable of delivering either water or foam. The figures used to describe the output of monitors vary widely and include litres per minute, gallons per minute, cubic metres per hour, and sometimes tons per hour; cubic metres per hour will be used here to give some indication of output. The output capacities required vary with the type of tug and the work that she does. Stringent specifications are laid down by oil terminal operators and this is reflected in requirements of the various international classification societies for vessels meeting particular standards. A common standard required of oil terminal tugs is known as "Fi Fi 1", which lays down certain parameters for pumping capacity, performance of the monitors and levels of protection for the tug itself. A typical oil terminal tug will have monitors capable of delivering between 200 and 600 cubic metres per hour of water each. The capacity when delivering foam will be considerably greater, but will vary with the density of the particular foam compound used. Oil rig supply vessels and some larger tugs working extensively in offshore oil fields are often equipped with fire monitors capable of delivering far in excess of those figures.

A modern high-capacity monitor is capable of throwing water to a height of over 150 metres when elevated at something like 45 degrees. In vessels where the monitors are mounted fairly low on the tug the height and distance achieved can be of great importance. Each monitor has a means of controlling the elevation and direction of the nozzle and in many designs the shape of the nozzle can also be adjusted. The monitors may be controlled manually, although it is now common for the entire outfit to be remotely controlled either from the wheelhouse or from a special control cabin. The remote controls are operated by hydraulic or electrical systems, or by turbine-driven mechanisms using water pressure from the fire-fighting system; the latter has the advantage of being unaffected by heat or moisture.

It is the manner in which the monitors are mounted, high above the vessel's superstructure, that gives a fire tug its distinctive appearance. Most tugs working with tankers will have at least one monitor mounted very high above the waterline, in order to be able to play water or foam over the ship's decks. With a very large tanker in ballast, the main deck may be over 18 metres above the waterline. It is not unusual, therefore, to have one monitor fitted at the tug's masthead approximately 21 metres above the waterline. There are a number of problems associated with having a relatively heavy fire monitor so high above the tug's deck; apart from any influence on stability, the effects of vibration and forces imposed

Fire fighting tug Eva Burrows *is equipped with a monitor on a telescopic mast with a capacity of 600 tonnes per hour. Two secondary monitors on the wheelhouse roof can deliver 180 tonnes per hour each. This Australian vessel also has a drenching system for self protection.* (Ship & Boat Int)

on the mast are considerable. The alternatives are to build substantial platforms or use a form of mounting that can be raised and lowered; both concepts have been used extensively in the past but are rarely found in new vessels.

The high towers, popular in the 1960s and 1970s, were mainly of tubular construction. They were light and strong but could also present problems of wind resistance and often ruined the appearance of the vessel. Variable height monitor mountings take two basic forms. The simplest and least obtrusive is the telescopic mast; a telescopic mechanism is usually incorporated inside a normal mast or a similar structure to house the tubular extending sections. Such masts can accommodate only one monitor and this may be of limited capacity. The second option is the hydraulically operated platform, similar to those used on land-based fire-fighting vehicles or for overhead maintenance. When not in use the platform folds down into a convenient stowage position. Platforms of this type are capable of carrying more weight than the telescopic kind and can be manned if required.

The use of fire-fighting foam is a common means of combating oil fires, and is used to blanket a fire by helping to exclude oxygen. It comprises a mixture of water, air and foam compound; the formulation of the compound varies, as does the proportion of water and compound, giving some control over the density of the resulting foam. The foam compound is automatically injected into the water supply, in carefully metered proportions, before it enters the monitor. Most monitors are capable of delivering approximately three or four times more foam than water. The foam compound is carried in specially designated tanks within the hull of the tug. As we have seen, the monitors are normally designed to handle water or foam, and in many fire-fighting operations only water will be used. Often when a tug is called to a shipboard fire her job will be to cool down the hull plating

Belfast fire tug Coleraine *has her main fire monitor mounted on a hydraulically operated elevating platform to enable it to reach above main deck level on very large ships.* Coleraine *is a single screw ship-handling tug of 212 gross tons and 32.2 metres in length owned by Cory Towage Ltd.* (Alan Geddes)

of other parts of the vessel's structure. Vast quantities of sea water are used, in operations which may take many hours. Hose connections fitted at deck level are used to enable additional hand-operated hoses to supplement the monitors if required and to enable fire-fighters to take hoses aboard the casualty.

Measures are also taken to protect the tug herself from the hazards of working in close proximity to fire. Reports of tugs working at major incidents mention scorched paintwork, cracked windows, and conditions too hot for men to work on deck. On some earlier tugs steel plates are provided, which can be erected to protect bridge windows. In most modern vessels a dousing, or wetting, system is installed. This consists of an arrangement of spray nozzles that continually envelop the vessel in a protective curtain of water. In order to prevent salt deposits building up on warm wheelhouse windows, the more sophisticated wetting systems use a separate fresh water supply for this part of the superstructure.

Pollution-control duties

As a direct result of public and political pressure, pollution-control measures in areas where major oil installations are located continue to become more stringent. Such measures generally comprise a comprehensive planned approach to preventing occurrences of significant oil pollution and ensuring that the means are in place to deal with any spill of oil should those measures fail. A great deal of effort and considerable resources are put into strict operating procedures and the provision of equipment to deal with such emergencies. The resident tug fleet and any purpose-built escort vessels inevitably become part of these "emergency response" arrangements; their availability and the ease with which they can be adapted to carry the necessary equipment has made them obvious candidates. Pollution-control duties involving tugs can be split broadly into three categories:

oil dispersal, containment, and retrieval. The extent of an oil spillage can vary from a small accidental discharge from a tanker in port, to a major incident involving thousands of tons of cargo released from a damaged vessel at sea. The type of oil discharged can also effect the treatment necessary. A light diesel fuel, which may evaporate relatively quickly, presents quite a different problem from a spill of heavy, tar-like crude oil. Huge advances in the development of equipment and pollution-control procedures have taken place in the last decade.

Oil dispersal

For many years the principal means of dealing with large- and small-scale oil pollution was to treat the offending slicks with a chemical dispersant, and such dispersal was carried out by tugs in a wide variety of circumstances, both at sea and in harbour. More recently it has been recognised that this method may in itself be environmentally unsound. In many areas chemical dispersant is used only under very strict control and guidance from local maritime authorities. Although dispersal is less popular, many tugs continue to be equipped to carry out the work.

In general the equipment carried on board a tug is intended to apply chemical dispersants and when necessary break up the slicks after the chemicals have done their work. Most fire-fighting tugs and many ordinary ship-handling vessels are capable of carrying several tons of chemical dispersant, in specially designated tanks. The spraying equipment used is sometimes permanently fitted and stowed in a convenient location on board, or removable and taken ashore when not required. The more complex arrangements consist of long tubular spraying arms rigged to extend outwards, one from each side of the tug; nozzles spaced along the arms discharge a spray of chemicals downwards on to the surface of the water, enabling the vessel to cover a wide path at each pass as it manoeuvres to cover the oil. For much smaller operations, such as small spillages in harbour, hand-operated spraying equipment may be used by crew members working from the tug's deck. These operations are time-consuming and require great patience from the tug crews.

The approach to breaking up oil slicks continues to change and several different methods are in use. A common method, still used in some

The escort tug Thorax, *owned by Johannes Ostensjo of Haugesund, has a bollard pull of 90 tonnes and is fully equipped to provide a number of emergency response duties. In this view the tug is about to deploy a boom from a reel on her boat deck. A skimmer (Framco 200 tonnes per hour) has been brought on deck from its garage ready for use and a workboat is being lowered to tend the boom.* (Johannes Ostensjo)

154

fleets, is to tow specially designed "breaker boards" through the oil. The boards are simple structures intended to cause a mixing action, agitating the surface of the oil and water. This method is particularly suitable for anti-pollution work at sea where very large areas have to be covered; some operators rely on the action of the tug's propellers to do the work. A further alternative method is to use the tug's fire monitors to direct high-pressure water jets at the surface.

Booms and oil retrieval

Pollution-control measures currently in use at many ports and oil terminals place great emphasis on the containment and retrieval of any oil spillage. In some parts of the world the use of a boom, a flexible floating barrier, is mandatory at oil terminals. Once a tanker is berthed a boom is put in position around the vessel before loading or unloading can commence. This is a safeguard against damaged hoses or other failures in the discharging equipment that may cause a spillage. Booms may also be used when an incident resulting in a release of oil occurs in sheltered waters; floating booms are used to contain the oil and prevent slicks being spread by the action of wind or tide. The boom is positioned around the damaged ship or oil slick as a barrier to contain the oil, and perhaps enable it to be retrieved. The use of booms at sea, even in relatively calm conditions, is quite a different matter due to the difficult task of keeping the lightweight booms in position against wind and tide.

Booms generally consist of a series of flexible floats assembled to form a long continuous barrier. A flexible rubber or canvas "skirt" is an integral part of the

Two more Ostensjo tugs, Audax *and* Vivax, *pictured taking part in an oil recovery exercise with a floating boom. Both tugs have their skimmers deployed from deck cranes to retrieve oil from the bight of the boom. The Foxtail skimmers in use have a capacity of 80 tonnes per hour and operate on the absorbent rope principle.* *(Johannes Ostensjo)*

boom and is arranged to extend a metre or so below the floats to help prevent the passage of oil. There are various designs in use including inflatable, fully portable types, which are stored on reels when not in use. Such booms are now becoming normal equipment for many tanker terminal tugs and escort vessels. A length of boom is usually contained on a reel stowed on the superstructure or at the forward end of the after towing deck, and deployed through an opening in the stern. As the boom is deployed the outer end is handled by a workboat or another tug. Booms that are in regular use at oil terminal berths are usually attended by purpose-built pollution-control craft, small tugs or workboats that tow booms into position and ensure that they are properly maintained.

Once an actual oil spill is contained by a boom it can be dealt with in two ways. The oil can be treated with a chemical dispersant, or steps may be taken to retrieve it. The latter procedure can be accomplished in very calm conditions by simply pumping the oil and surface water into tanks. The resulting water/oil solution is allowed to settle and taken ashore for treatment. This very basic method of removing oil from the surface of the water has, however, been superseded by far more sophisticated means. Among devices designed to remove only the oil, with a minimum of water content, are rotating mops that soak up oil and various skimming devices. A skimmer of some kind is again becoming standard equipment on tugs involved in pollution-control duties, and is housed aboard the tug and lowered by a deck crane into the oil contained by the boom. Hoses connect the skimming device to pumps aboard the tug where the water/oil solution is stored in specially allocated settling tanks.

An alternative retrieval method is to have a short length of boom rigged from one or both sides of the tug, with its outer end suspended by a long lightweight spar. The boom is rigged so that a bight is formed when the tug moves slowly forward, and any oil on the surface is collected at the after end of the bight, then a skimmer is lowered into the bight to retrieve the oil as previously described.

Active anti-pollution measures such as spraying with dispersant, breaking up slicks by agitation or retrieval require precise knowledge of the position, size and movement of known oil slicks, and in many modern vessels, electronic charting and positioning equipment is installed for just this purpose. The position of slicks can be shown graphically on the VDU screen along with the real-time position of the tug. The direction in which the oil is likely to drift can be predicted and search patterns depicted on the screen.

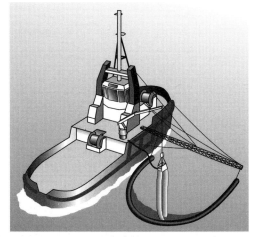

The side sweep oil recovery method enables the tug to manouvre to collect oil in the bight of a boom suspended from the light weight arm carried on board. A skimmer is shown lowered into the bight to recover any accumulated oil.

Tugs for ice-breaking

The use of tugs for ice-breaking is a duty far removed from those previously described, but there are still several common factors. There are many harbours and coastal waters that for some weeks or months each year can only be kept open to shipping by the use of some form of ice-breaker. In many cases the expense of a purpose-built vessel dedicated to this seasonal work is not justified, but the use of a suitably designed tug, to be employed principally as a ship-handling vessel, is a different matter. In North America, Northern Europe, Scandinavia and Russia there are many such tugs; some are employed to keep harbours, their approaches and coastal shipping lanes open as small ice-breakers in their own right, often dealing with ice over 300 mm thick. Others are strengthened and equipped simply to enable them to continue about their normal business of assisting ships, unimpeded by ice.

A third and more recent category of ice-breaking tug is the large deep-sea vessel used for specialist towing duties by the oil industry. Offshore oil exploration has moved north into ice-infested areas such as Alaska, and much of the equipment used in these northern oil fields is transported by barges towed by purpose-built ice-strengthened tugs. The same principles apply broadly to all such vessels.

The main constructional difference between an ice-breaking tug and any other lies in the strength and shape of the hull. The need for additional strength is obvious; the hull must resist not only the forces imposed by her forward motion

Swedish tug Per *from the fleet of Roda Bolaget is pictured working in ice, a duty common for many tug fleets operating in northern ports.* Per *is an ice breaking, coastal and harbour tug of 3410 bhp built in 1972.* (*Roda Bolaget*)

through ice, but also any crushing that may take place. Additional strength is introduced by using thicker steel plating and increasing the number of supporting internal frames, and the bow of the tug normally has a long, shallow, angled portion just below the waterline. In order to appreciate the purpose of this strange shape, the principle of ice-breaking must be understood. The tug breaks ice not by battering it with brute force but by riding up over it and using her weight to do the work. The long sloping shape aids this process and acts as a form of cutting edge. There may also be a more rounded shape in the body of the hull to minimise the risk of the tug becoming "squeezed" or crushed; a more rounded shape will simply be forced upwards if crushing occurs.

Other considerations concern the propulsion system. Many modern ice-breaking or strengthened tugs have been fitted with conventional open propellers; nozzles are often avoided due to the risk of ice becoming jammed between the propeller blades and nozzle structure. Small protruding fins are often located ahead of the propeller and aft of the rudder to deflect ice away from those vital components. A number of tractor tugs with azimuthing propulsion units are successfully employed in Scandinavian fleets; their propulsion equipment appears to be unaffected by ice, presumably due to the deep immersion of their propellers.

The cooling systems for the main and auxiliary engines may also be modified in order to be operated without circulating sea water from outside the hull, thus avoiding problems resulting from frozen or blocked water intakes. Closed circuit cooling systems are used, utilising internal water tanks and the surface plating of the hull to provide the necessary dissipation of heat.

The Russian built twin screw tug Capt I B Harvey *is unlikely to encounter ice in her home port of Swansea in South Wales but she has been designed to work in ice. Seen here in heavy weather, the underwater shape of her ice breaking bow is clearly visible. She is one of several similar 1600 bhp tugs from the fleet of West Coast Towing (UK) Ltd.* (Danny Lynch)

CHAPTER 8

Ocean-going tugs and offshore support vessels

Tugs in this category include the largest and most impressive vessels of all. Among them are the massive sea-going vessels involved in long-distance towing and salvage work, and anchor-handling tugs and oil rig supply vessels involved in supporting the offshore oil industry.

The sector of the towage industry in which most of these vessels work has undergone major economic and operational change in the past decade. Demand for tugs built specifically to carry out salvage work and long-range towing operations, with ships and other large floating objects, has dropped dramatically. Conversely, the market for large, powerful vessels capable of anchor-handling and other duties in the offshore oil industry is considerably more active. This has resulted in a massive slimming down of fleets consisting mainly of salvage tugs of the more traditional designs; large numbers of such vessels have been sold for scrap or a variety of other uses, decimating several well-known fleets.

A deep-sea tug of any type represents a massive investment for her owners in terms of capital and operating costs. In order to survive in present towage markets a vessel must be capable of providing a wide range of services in a highly competitive industry. In the present economic climate this often means a vessel with an open stern, a good towing capability and with at least some cargo capacity. This may be a versatile anchor-handling tug or perhaps a purpose-built, well-equipped, anchor-handling oil rig supply vessel.

Deep-sea tugs and oil rig supply vessels are generally owned by major towage companies or specialist companies involved in oil industry support services. Among the latter are a number of relatively new firms operating modern, highly sophisticated ships. Many well-known names, synonymous with ocean towing, such as Bugsier, Moran, Smit, Svitzer, Tsavliris and Wysmuller continue to be deeply involved in the industry. Market conditions have, however, forced many to enter into joint ventures, or pool resources in other ways in order to maintain a share of the available business. The European and American companies mentioned face vigorous competition from Singapore, South Africa, the Middle East, Japan and, increasingly, Russia.

Following the dissolution of the former USSR a great many ocean-going tugs and oil rig supply vessels were released into the commercial market in order to earn badly needed foreign currency. These vessels continue to provide stiff competition, due mainly to their low manning costs. Several Russian vessels have

Oceanic is the sole surviving vessel of her type in what was once one of the world's largest and most modern fleets of deep sea tugs. Owned by Bugsier Reederei of Hamburg, she is a twin screw tug of 2047 gross tons and 13200 bhp built in 1969 to a largely traditional design. In spite of many modifications the future of this vessel (in 1995) remains tenuous. (Bugsier Reederei)

One of many Russian owned vessels trading widely in the commercial market is the anchor handling tug Neftegaz-62. Built in Poland in 1989, she is a twin screw vessel of 2723 gross tons and 8640 bhp with a bollard pull of 75 tonnes. (Ray Johnson)

joined established western fleets, on charter or as part of joint operating arrangements.

Most of the navies of the world continue to operate deep-sea tugs for rescue and support purposes, but rarely become involved in commercial towing.

Ocean-going tugs

"Ocean-going" or "deep-sea" are both terms used to describe tugs intended primarily to operate at sea and undertake long-range towing operations. They vary in size from a vessel little larger than a harbour tug, of 35 metres in length and perhaps 350 tons gross, to massive vessels of almost 100 metres long and over 5,000 tons gross. Anchor-handling tugs, employed largely by the offshore oil industry, also belong in this category, but are equipped in a particular way for the work that they do; the special equipment required and the process of anchor-handling is dealt with later in this chapter. As already mentioned, the oil rig supply vessel is increasingly being used to carry out work that was previously the prime role of the traditional ocean-going tug. There are, however, significant numbers of the latter still in use, and it is with those that the next few paragraphs are mainly concerned.

The ability to operate at sea in almost all weather conditions is a most important feature of any ocean-going tug. To some degree the ability to withstand extremely bad sea states and very high winds is dependent on the size of the vessel. A large tug is, in every respect, a small ship, capable of withstanding the very worst weather conditions and with sufficient range to undertake extremely long voyages. In almost every case the hull design incorporates a high forecastle to afford maximum protection in heavy seas, and some form of protection along her sides to guard against heavy knocks when working alongside other vessels. This usually takes the form of an external steel rubbing band, with perhaps some

Sirocco and Sumatras are from a fleet of seven similar tugs operated by the Dutch company International Transport Contractors BV. Built to a traditional design in 1976/77 they are twin screw tugs of 847 gross tons and 110 tonnes bollard pull, with main engines of 9029 bhp. Note the "crowsnest" style upper wheelhouse. (ITC)

diagonal reinforcement. Bow fenders are of limited use in many of the very large tugs and can be a distinct disadvantage in heavy seas.

The superstructure in earlier designs tends to follow the traditional tug configuration, with the wheelhouse and bridge very close to the bow. This may necessitate a secondary control position further aft (often known among tugmen as a "dog house") to give the tug master a better view astern when manoeuvring or picking up a tow. A control position of this kind often comprises a completely separate wheelhouse equipped with engine, steering and winch controls. Another form of additional control position is the "crow's nest", a very small wheelhouse located high above the normal superstructure. A number of ocean-going tugs are equipped in this way to afford improved all-round vision when the tug is towing, searching for a casualty, or working her way through ice.

More recent vessels have a single wheelhouse located almost amidships, in a position giving a good field of view in all directions. Duplicate controls are provided at windows facing aft with a clear view of the towing deck. The towing winches in many of the larger vessels are located within the superstructure and are frequently of the friction type. Because this arrangement is out of sight from the wheelhouse, closed circuit television is often fitted to monitor the movement of the towline passing round the various winch drums, thus avoiding a serious problem from fouled or jammed rope.

The propulsion system fitted in the vast majority of large ocean-going tugs will be of the conventional screw type, incorporating some form of propulsion nozzle.

The Russian owned Fotiy Krylov *remains one of the world's largest and most powerful salvage tugs. Now operated by Tsavliris-Russ (Worldwide Salvage & Towage) Ltd of Greece, she has four main engines driving twin controllable pitch propellers with a total of 24480 bhp to give a bollard pull of 248 tonnes and maximum speed of 19.5 knots. Registered as 5250 gross tons and 99 metres in length, she carries a massive array of towing and salvage equipment.* (Author)

Smit Rotterdam *is one of a number of ocean going tugs operated in the livery of SmitWijs, a consortium formed by Smith International and Bureau Wysmuller to compete for towage and salvage work on the world market. The tug was built in 1975, a vessel of 2650 gross tons and 74.75 metres in length, powered by main engines of 13500 bhp to give a bollard pull of 167 tonnes. In this shot the tug has the oil rig Ocean Valiant in tow.* (Fotoflite)

Twin-screw vessels with fixed nozzles and controllable-pitch propellers are the most common in current fleets, each propeller being driven by one or two engines. Power output will of course depend to some degree on the size of vessel, and can vary from around 3,000 bhp to a massive 25,000 bhp; the latter is the rating given to a pair of Russian-built tugs currently operating on the commercial towage and salvage market. Bollard pull performance will also vary between approximately 40 tons and the 248 tonnes produced by those very large vessels. Free running speed is more important in ocean-going tugs than most other types – the need to reach a casualty or the next task quickly is of the essence, and may determine the success or failure of an operation. Speeds of up to 18 knots can be achieved by some of the larger vessels.

The handling characteristics of deep-sea tugs have to meet requirements rather different from the smaller vessels mentioned in previous chapters. Their ability to handle well at sea, with perhaps an ungainly vessel in tow, is more important than extreme agility. Manoeuvrability remains important, however, particularly in tugs conducting salvage operations and working in the offshore oil industry. The installation of a powerful transverse bow thruster is one of the most popular aids to improved manoeuvrability, and stern thrusters are also becoming common in offshore anchor-handlers. Integrated control systems are also used extensively to simplify the handling of larger tugs while working in close proximity to other craft and offshore installations (see the section on Integrated control systems in Chapter 2).

A comprehensive outfit of towing gear is installed. The sheer size of the winches and towlines of a very large tug surprises many people. The main steel wire tow ropes on many large deep-sea tugs are between 180 and 230 mm in circumference with a length of approximately 1,200 metres. Sufficient spare gear is carried to enable towing connections to be made using shorter lengths of wire rope, chain cable, and possibly large-diameter nylon rope springs. Smaller tugger winches are fitted handle tow ropes and bridles and to assist in setting up towing gear or ground tackle.

Salvage

The subject of salvage is an extremely wide one, on which many books have been written. The material that follows is intended only to give an indication of the work that salvage tugs must be prepared and equipped to carry out. Very few tugs are now employed solely in the traditional salvage role. Up to 20 years ago it was common for many fully equipped tugs to be stationed in strategic locations around the world, where long periods were spent waiting to intercept a radio message indicating that a ship was in difficulties and required assistance. The rising cost of tugs and manpower has rendered this type of operation prohibitive for most owners, and the vessels engaged in this kind of salvage work are often subsidised, either by the owners themselves or by funds from government sources.

The fact remains that ships still suffer machinery breakdowns, weather damage or fires, and they still run aground. In most cases a well-equipped tug is required to give assistance or if necessary carry out a full-scale salvage operation. A ship would be very fortunate indeed to have such a tug awaiting her calls at a nearby salvage station – one is far more likely to be diverted from work elsewhere or dispatched from her home port. A number of serious accidents in recent years,

Heavy weather off the coast of South Africa in 1994 ripped away part of the bow of the tanker Tochal, *a tanker of 300,078 tons dwt. The ship was attended by tugs from the fleet of Pentow Marine, including the 4000 bhp anchor-handling supply vessel* Pentow Salvor *(bearing her original name* Rockfish *in the picture).* (Pentow)

Government agencies in a number of countries have sponsored large tugs or other suitable vessels to be stationed in vulnerable areas in a stand-by role. Brodospas Moon is one such vessel, employed by the British Coastguard to patrol the English Channel and southern approaches during the winter months of 1994/95. She is an anchor-handling tug supply vessel of 8648 bhp with a bollard pull of 102 tonnes. (Author)

where marine pollution has become a prominent issue, have persuaded several governments to fund the provision of salvage vessels in a "stand-by role" at sensitive locations. The areas affected are those where shipping lanes are exceptionally busy, where a high proportion of hazardous cargoes are being carried, or where the coastline is particularly inhospitable and the weather unpredictable. In some cases salvage tugs or other suitable vessels are contracted to provide cover all year round, and in others for the winter months when weather conditions are poor. The duty of a "stand-by vessel" is to attend the casualty as quickly as possible and render whatever assistance is necessary, the priority being to prevent the ship foundering and/or becoming a pollution hazard. Such vessels are generally under the direct control of the Coastguard or other government agency. Among the countries operating "stand-by" services are Britain, France, the Netherlands and South Africa.

There remains a romantic notion that successful salvage operations produce rich rewards for owners and crews alike. While this is still occasionally the case, salvage specialists will argue that the massive costs of spectacular and difficult operations are rarely met by the resulting remuneration. This has resulted in a marked decline in the interest shown in salvage by some major operators. For many years the industry has relied heavily on "Lloyds Standard Form of Salvage Agreement – No Cure No Pay", often known as "Lloyds Open Form" (LOF), to ensure a fair and just settlement of salvage claims. This agreement, once made between tug and ship owners, enables salvage operations to take place immediately without the need for complicated financial negotiations before work can start. When the operation is completed, a salvage award is eventually decided

The tanker Freja Svea *is shown aground on the north east coast of Britain in 1993. the 12728 bhp anchor-handling tug supply vessel* Solfonn *is making a towing connection in a heavy ground swell. The picture, taken through the bridge windows, shows the towline passing between two hydraulically operated stop pins.* *(Howard Smith T&S)*

by an arbitration committee at Lloyds of London. If the salvage attempt fails, no payment is made. In these days of improved communications other arrangements or agreements may be possible. The use of facsimile and secure radio transmission enables negotiations to take place and a contract to be made privately in a very short time. "Lloyds Open Form" is still widely used in emergency situations where a ship is in danger and little time is available to make other arrangements.

A major concern of the present-day salvor is the question of financial liability should a major pollution incident result from a salvage operation or occur while the casualty is in his charge. Stringent regulations and constraints are imposed by local authorities and marine agencies on the movement of damaged ships into coastal waters, and many place huge responsibilities on the salvage company. Thus the financial risk to the salvor and insurers is considerable and may deter smaller operators from becoming involved in the more difficult salvage operations.

The term "salvage tug" is applied loosely to any vessel capable of carrying out the work in hand, but it is generally accepted to be one equipped to a certain standard. A successful salvage tug must be self-sufficient to a large extent. She will be large enough and have adequate power to assist casualties in a variety of different circumstances, often in remote parts of the world; the size of ship requiring a tow may be a vessel of up to half a million tons. Tankers or bulk cargo carriers of huge proportions have required assistance from time to time due to propulsion or steering system failures and damage caused by heavy weather. Although the first tug to reach a very large casualty may not be sufficiently powerful to deal with it unaided, she may be used to prevent the ship from drifting into danger or render other assistance.

In Chapter 6, dealing with ship-handling, the process of "picking up" a tow was described as one requiring a great deal of skill. When an ocean-going tug is required to carry out the same procedure the hazards are multiplied. If the tug is called to a damaged ship in heavy seas, getting the tug in close enough pass a towline in the usual manner, by heaving line, may be impossible. In high winds a ship without power may be drifting considerably and there are a number of alternative methods of making a connection. A line may be fired over the vessel using a rocket gun, or floated downwind towards the vessel using a small buoy or float.

In order to simplify the business of taking ships in tow quickly in an emergency, international maritime organisations are advocating the installation of emergency towing equipment in all vessels above a certain size. The equipment called for is normally located at the stern of the ship and can take several forms. In general it comprises a steel wire towline or man-made fibre rope, stowed on a reel or in a special sealed container. The inner end of the wire is securely fastened to a towing point on the ship and the outer to a long messenger line and a small coloured buoy. In the case of an emergency, the buoy and messenger line are thrown overboard by the crew to float away from the ship, for retrieval by the tug. The tug then hauls in the messenger line to pull the towline from its stowage.

There may also be difficulties when the casualty is aground in relatively shallow water – a tug may not be able to approach due to her own deep draught. In good conditions a boat can be used, but in poor weather line guns, floats or other methods may have to be tried. To assist a ship aground the tug may require additional anchors and sufficient towing gear to make up "ground tackles", a method of increasing the tug's pulling capacity by using anchors and a multiple pulley system. The casualty may be damaged and require temporary repairs to her

In order to successfully remove the grounded bulk carrier Sea Transporter *from the shore of Goa, in India, Smit International cut the ship in two parts. Here the bow section is being towed clear by the anchor-handling supply vessel* Smit-Lloyd 71, *leaving the after portion to be refloated later.*   (Smit)

hull. For this work diving, welding and cutting equipment will be needed and a supply of materials. Once repaired, the ship may have to be pumped out using pumps from the tug and perhaps portable units transported from shore. In more complex operations compressed air may be used to gain buoyancy and drive water from internal compartments. The need to discharge all or part of a ship's cargo before she can be refloated is a common occurrence. Electrical power may be needed to enable the ship's cranes to be used; if her engine room is flooded, or out of action for other reasons, power will be supplied either by the tug's generators or by transferring portable units. Where a large and badly damaged ship, such as a tanker, is aground it may be necessary to cut the vessel into two or more parts and refloat each component separately. This is often done with the careful use of small explosive charges. These are common salvage tasks that may have to be carried out in remote parts of the world where little outside assistance is available.

Fire aboard ship is one of the most serious hazards for the mariner and presents particular problems for the salvor. The fire may be fought using monitors and equipment installed aboard the tug similar to that described in Chapter 7. But fires are not necessarily extinguished by simply dousing them with foam or water. Engine room fires, caused by broken fuel pipes and similar failures, are perhaps the most common occurrence. These are necessarily fought on board the ship, and in this scenario the tug is likely to be tasked with cooling down the exterior of the hull and superstructure to prevent the fire spreading and minimise structural damage. Cargo vessels with complicated stowage arrangements may have deep-seated fires needing other methods to extinguish them, such as injecting carbon dioxide gas. Bulk cargoes of grain, coal and other combustible materials suffer problems with spontaneous combustion and are particularly difficult to extinguish. Flooding the ship with water to extinguish a fire may be the only solution, but considerable thought has to be given to her stability. It may be necessary to beach the vessel on a suitable shore or take other precautions to prevent her capsizing due to the weight of water used in fire-fighting.

Collision is probably the most common cause of shipping casualties, particularly in heavily congested coastal waters. The damage inflicted in a collision between two ships can vary dramatically from minor indentations to a vessel being virtually cut in two. Flooding, due to damage below the waterline, may be contained by pumping until a safe haven can be reached, or alternatively some form of temporary repair may be necessary. Once damage to the hull has been temporarily repaired it may be necessary to tow the vessel to port. Towage operations are carefully planned to avoid further damage; it is not unusual for a damaged ship to be towed stern-first or at a particularly low speed to reduce the pressure on bulkheads and other parts of a weakened hull structure.

Long-distance towing

Long-distance towing can be conveniently split into two types of operation, the towage of conventional ships and operations involving the towage of a wide variety of other floating objects.

Towing ships over long distances is a traditional activity that has changed little in concept since tugs first went to sea. However, the size of ships likely to be towed has grown dramatically, and it must be accepted that any ship currently in service

Sister tugs Sirocco *and* Sumatras *are pictured towing the tanker* Avat *from Le Havre to Cadiz. Both tugs have a separate towline connected to the ship. Once clear of the congested western approaches a single tug continued alone to tow the ship to its final destination in the Arabian Gulf.* (ITC)

may require towage at sea at some stage. Thus many ocean-going tugs now in service can deal efficiently with ships of any size. Ships are towed long distances for a number of reasons. Even the most modern vessel can be disabled by a machinery failure and require towage to a suitable shipyard for repair. Ship-repairing and reconstruction is an extremely competitive business and ships are towed many thousands of miles to have work carried out. In the same way, new ships may have their hulls built in one location and be fitted out many thousands of miles away for sound economic reasons. Old and redundant ships, sold for breaking up, are towed to parts of the world offering the best prices for scrap steel. The cost of towage is part of the economic equation, and competition for such work is fierce. A very large tug, properly equipped, has been known to tow two, three or even four ships at a time to shipbreakers in the Far East from Europe, the USA and South America.

Towage operations concerned with other kinds of floating object can be considerably more complex. As the towage industry has developed, the subjects for transport by towing have become larger and stranger. Large pieces of floating plant, dredgers, cranes, oil drilling rigs and similar items are frequently towed long distances in the conventional way; the products of heavy engineering are often too large and unwieldy to be shipped in any other way. Many of these objects are slow, difficult tows requiring great care, and are particularly vulnerable in very bad weather conditions, but in the last decade or so "dry towing" has eliminated some of those difficulties.

"Dry towing" refers to the transportation of such objects by loading them on to a very large barge. In order to allow large pieces of floating equipment to be loaded the barges are designed to be temporarily submerged. The buoyancy of the barge is controlled by pumping and ballasting systems located beneath the single flat deck. Once the barge is submerged, the object to be transported is towed into position over the deck, the barge is then raised and the object secured – usually by welding it temporarily to the deck. In this way complete oil rigs and similar pieces of equipment can be loaded and towed more safely and often much faster than would be possible if they were afloat. Dredging companies make good use of this method of transport; a whole dredging outfit – dredgers, dump barges, floating pipelines, and small dredging tugs – are often loaded on to one barge. Once secured, the entire outfit can be towed to a new location, on the other side of the world if necessary.

The transport of large or awkward "non-floating" items by barge is now commonplace. Flat-topped pontoon barges are normally used, some of which are very large, to carry items such as dockside cranes, sections for new bridges, huge oil refinery components, and fabricated sections of new ships. Offshore oil and gas production facilities, under construction many miles from shore, frequently have much of their upperworks and machinery built in modular form at engineering yards ashore. Individual modules, some weighing many hundreds of tonnes, are transported by barge to the construction site and lifted into place. Bulk commodities such as stone, coal, ore, petroleum products, timber and paper are also transported long distances by tug and barge in large quantities. The barges used in this work can vary in size up to a carrying capacity of 20,000 tons or larger.

The economics of any towage operation are governed not only by the cost of hiring suitable tugs but also by the expense of insuring both tug and tow. The premium for a major towage operation is based on many factors. Specialist companies are often used to assess the risks, taking into account the type of tug, the nature of the vessel to be towed, the distance, route, and likely weather conditions. Recommendations may be made and conditions laid down regarding towing methods, the route, and the way the tow is to be conducted. The matter of insurance and relatively lower risks have been partially responsible for the success of "dry towing". Unfortunately for the tug owner, the "dry towing" method faces stiff competition from the operators of self-propelled heavy-lift vessels offering similar services.

"Dry towing" was selected as the most suitable method of transporting the "jack up" rig Zapata Scotia *from Singapore to Halifax. The rig is shown here loaded aboard the submersible pontoon barge* Seacamel 393-12. *(ITC)*

Towing operations

The principles involved in towing over long distances are much the same as those previously described for coastal

The flat topped pontoon barge AMT Traveller *(9779 tonnes cargo capacity) is typical of many used to transport a wide range of unwieldy items by sea. Clearly visible is the chain bridle, secured to "Smit brackets" aboard the barge (inset) and an emergency towline fastened along the side below deck level. The bridle is part of the barge's equipment and may be hauled aboard by a small winch in the bow.* (Author)

towing – only the scale of the operation differs. Preparations for a tow are made in exactly the same manner. The vessel to be towed is surveyed and any necessary steps taken to ensure that it remains seaworthy for the duration of the voyage. Ships, oil rigs and similar vessels may have a small "running crew" on board to care for the towing connections, pumps and lighting, and generally to monitor the condition of the vessel. Provision is made for this small crew to be housed as comfortably as possible, in what may be somewhat austere conditions. Once the tow is at sea their only contact with the tug will be by radio.

A critical factor as always is the towing connection, and considerable attention is paid to the towline and its connections. Many large barges and some ships have special fittings permanently welded to their decks to enable towing connections to be made swiftly and efficiently. These are known as "Smit brackets" and were developed by the Dutch towing specialists Smit International, as part of a study to develop quick and efficient methods of taking large vessels in tow. The Smit bracket allows the eye end of a towline or bridle to be secured quickly by a large sliding pin. A bridle is usually made up from lengths of chain cable, or steel wire, coupled to the towline to form a "Y". The two legs of the bridle are then secured aboard the vessel to be towed. The bridles used on very large barges that are in constant use are extremely heavy and designed to resist the constant wear and chafing that takes place during towing.

When taking a ship in tow a chain bridle or the ship's own anchor cable are commonly used to make the towing connection. The anchor is generally removed from the cable and the towline connected in its place. A few metres of cable are then paid out, making a durable and effective connection. Alternatively, the anchor can be disconnected but left in place in the hawse pipe and the cable paid out through a suitable fairlead in the ship's bow.

Prior to leaving port an emergency towline will be rigged aboard the vessel to be towed. This takes the form of a length of steel wire towrope secured at one end to bitts on board the vessel, arranged along her sides or rails and held in place by rope lashings. To the free end of this emergency towline is coupled a length of rope and a small brightly coloured buoy. Once the tug and tow are under way the buoy and its line are thrown overboard to trail astern of the convoy. If the main towline should break during bad weather, the tug can rapidly locate the buoy and, using the light line, haul the end of the emergency towline on board and make it secure. As the tug takes up a towing position the remainder of the emergency towline breaks free from its lashings and extends to its full length.

In many tows a length of large-diameter nylon rope will be used to connect the main towline to the bridle or cable, to act as a "spring" to help cushion the towline against shock loading. On board the tug some provision may also be necessary to ensure that the towline is protected against chafing. In the more modern vessels the tug's stern is designed to avoid contact with the towing gear, but where this is not the case the towline will be protected by rubber sleeves or the contact points heavily greased.

Once an ocean-going tug and her tow are at sea the main towline will be adjusted to a length suitable for the conditions, being paid out by the winch to several hundreds of metres in length. An important feature of the towline in deep-sea operations is its inherent sag or catenary. The length and weight of the towline act as a spring or damper, lessening the effects of snatching and shock loadings caused by the action of the waves and the relative motion of both vessels. A steel towline several hundred metres in length will sag considerably and remain

Anchor-handling tug Anglian Duke *is seen manoeuvring to leave port with 20,000 tonne barge rigged to transport rock between Norway and Britain.* Anglian Duke *was built in 1977 and is a tug of 498 gross tons and 8400 bhp, with a bollard pull of 80 tonnes, owned by Klyne Tugs Ltd of Lowestoft.* (Author)

The "jack up" oil drilling rig Britannia is entering the river Humber for repairs in tow of the anchor-handling tug Tempest *and the anchor-handling supply vessel* Smit Lloyd Safe – *a typical duty for either vessel.* Tempest *is a tug of 9350 bhp with a bollard pull of 120 tonnes and* Smit Lloyd Safe *has 8000 bhp with 115 tonnes bollard pull.*   (Specialist Marine Services)

deeply submerged. When the tug enters busy coastal sea lanes the tow will be shortened to give the tug master better control and ensure that the towline does not foul the seabed. Alternatively, in poor weather the towline may be lengthened further to reduce the strain on the towing connections.

When more than one vessel is to be towed, if at all possible a separate towline will be used for each. For example, if two ships are towed, a towline will be rigged for each from separate drums on the towing winch. This enables the respective towline lengths to be adjusted so that the vessels will not collide with each other or foul the towlines. There are occasions when it is necessary to tow in tandem, with one vessel connected to another. This presents difficulties for the tug master in that he has little control of the towline between the two vessels; its length cannot be adjusted when entering harbour or for different weather conditions.

There are also many occasions when more than one tug will be required to handle a particular tow. If two tugs are engaged to tow a large vessel over long distances, separate towlines will be connected directly to the vessel. The length of the towlines will be adjusted and the position of each tug monitored carefully during the voyage to minimise the risk of collision and ensure that the towing loads are equally distributed. Very large tows, for example the positioning of permanent oil production platforms, may involve a whole fleet of tugs. The platforms are usually constructed at sheltered, coastal sites, towed to their final location offshore and lowered into position by flooding parts of the structure. The tugs used for such an operation are selected by size, bollard pull, and handling characteristics. Each is connected to a particular position on the structure and the entire operation is controlled by a "tow master" from a vantage point on board. The tow master co-ordinates the movement of all the tugs to achieve the correct course and speed.

A less common towing method, used occasionally as a temporary expedient, is towing in tandem. A towing connection is made from the winch or tow hook of one tug to the bow of the other. This method is sometimes used when additional power is required to assist another tug in difficulties or when refloating a ship aground. Provided that the first tug has a towline of suitable strength, it is a simple means of adding more power without the need to make another towing connection. A temporary tandem towing connection is sometimes made when a tug makes a rendezvous with another tug and its tow to transfer fuel or fresh water. In this situation hoses, etc, can be hauled along the towline.

Far Centurion is an anchor-handling oil rig supply vessel of 1599 gross tons built in Korea in 1983. Operated by Far Shipping A/S she has four main engines driving twin screw propellers with a total of 13040 bhp. This arrangement gives her a bollard pull of 151 tonnes and a free running speed of over 15 knots. (Author)

Anchor-handling tugs and oil rig supply vessels

These vessels perform duties that are arduous and often dangerous, and in order to satisfy the current demands of the offshore oil industry they must be able to participate in towing, positioning and anchoring the current range of drilling rigs, pipe-laying barges, and similar pieces of floating plant, and keep them supplied with consumable stores. The offshore oil industry continues to probe more remote locations and is now operating in deeper waters and in increasingly hostile climates. To undertake this work the size of rigs and plant in general has also increased. Consequently, the vessels required to assist in these operations have, of necessity, become larger and more powerful.

Any major offshore rig or similar piece of plant will be supported by a number of vessels. If the rig or barge is of the "jack-up" type it will be towed into position and the supporting legs jacked down to raise it above the surface of the water. Such a rig will then only require the services of a supply ship and a stand-by vessel. The oil rig

Oil exploration rigs of the semi-submersible type, such as the Ocean Nomad, are towed long distances at sea but on arrival at the drilling site must be securely anchored. The rig's anchors are visible around the bottom of the 'legs. Ocean Nomad is shown under tow at a good speed behind the tug Smit Singapore *a 1350 bhp vessel with a 189 tonnes bollard pull.* (Smit)

supply vessel will attend regularly to deliver supplies and remove unwanted waste and equipment. A standby vessel is a mandatory requirement in most locations and is constantly on station to ensure that other shipping remains a safe distance from the rig and to assist in emergency situations, such as the evacuation of a rig. Occasionally a suitably equipped tug or supply vessel will be used to perform the duties of a stand-by vessel.

Rigs and construction vessels of the semi-submersible type remain afloat and need to be anchored when they arrive in the selected location; most of those used by the offshore oil industry are moored using a system of eight or ten anchors deployed in a star-shaped pattern. Each of these anchors must be taken out in turn to an exact position and lowered to the seabed. Rig anchors weigh in the order of 12–16 tons, or larger in some special cases. When the rig moves the anchors have to be "broken out" of the seabed, raised, and carried back to the rig, and these anchor-handling tasks will be carried out by a team of anchor-handling tugs or oil rig supply vessels. While the rig is in position it requires much the same stand-by and supply services as the jack-up type. Anchor-handling tugs, without a substantial cargo capacity, remain with a rig only if further moves are to be made quite frequently. In the case of a pipe-laying barge, the tugs remain in use constantly, relaying anchors every few hours as the barge moves forward.

The anchor-handling tug

The modern anchor-handler is a powerful, well-equipped deep-sea tug embodying many of the features of a traditional deep-sea tug and always an open stern. She will almost certainly be a twin-screw vessel with Kort nozzles and probably controllable-pitch propellers. At least one transverse thruster and an integrated control system are common features on this type of vessel, which spends much of its working life in close proximity to other craft. The size and power of an anchor-handler varies, but vessels of approximately 500 tons gross and 6,000 bhp are common and economical in terms of manning. There are many larger and more powerful vessels.

To enable her to handle the heavy and unwieldy anchors effectively the tug must have a completely clear afterdeck and a winch designed for the purpose. During the anchor-handling process the tug is often required to take the anchors on board by hauling them over her stern, along with their associated chain and other fittings. For this purpose a large, heavily constructed horizontal roller is installed in the stern, usually at deck level. To prevent damage to the deck, a thick wooden cladding is applied to the working area. Guard rails are often fitted at either side of the working area to afford some protection to the crew and prevent fouling should an anchor break loose in heavy weather.

Husky is a tug from the fleet of Heerema Marine Contractors capable of anchor-handling and towing. She was built in Holland in 1978, a vessel of 1533 gross tons powered by two main engines producing a total of 12000 bhp. She is a well equipped tug with a bollard pull of 152 tonnes and a free running speed of 15 knots. (Author)

This stern view of the anchor-handling tug Angian Earl *shows her open stern and the fendering around her forecastle and sides. In this shot she has a typical after control position "dog house" (now removed).* Anglian Earl *is a vessel of 665 gross tons and 5750 bhp, with a 84 tonnes bollard pull, built in Belgium in 1976.* (Author)

The winch in an anchor-handling tug has at least two drums, with one designed specially for hauling up anchors and capable of producing a static pull much higher than that required for towing. The wire rope fitted to that drum is likely to be shorter than a towing wire, but must be of sufficient strength to withstand the strain of breaking an anchor from the seabed and bringing it aboard. In order to simplify the work of securing the anchors and their chain cables, and reduce the workload of crewmen on the exposed afterdeck, special handling equipment has been developed. This equipment varies, but generally consists of some form of jaw or gripping device. This is located near the stern of the vessel, ahead of the stern roller, and retracts flush with the deck when not in use. The "Sharks jaw", "Karmfork" and "Triplex" are all well-known types of line- and chain-handling equipment. Most comprise a hydraulically operated jaw or other device that rises vertically from the deck to grip the chain or wire of a rig anchor securely once it has been hauled on board over the stern roller. These devices are normally used in conjunction with at least two hydraulically operated

177

stop pins; a common arrangement is to have two gripping devices, each served by a pair of stop pins.

The work of handling heavy anchors, chain, buoys and other equipment on the afterdeck is aided by the use of at least two tugger winches. Wires from these winches are used in conjunction with various fairleads around the after end of the vessel to move heavy items around. A versatile hydraulic deck crane with a useful working capacity of 10–20 tons is invaluable aboard the anchor-handler and found on virtually every vessel. An ability to carry some cargo on the afterdeck has also proved an advantage when working offshore. The cargo often takes the form of standard international-size containers. These may contain stores of some kind, or be fitted out for some special operation such as diving or surveying. It is in this area that the dividing line between the anchor-handling tug and oil rig supply vessel is becoming increasingly blurred.

Oil rig supply vessels
There are several types of oil rig supply vessel in use in offshore oil fields throughout the world. They can be divided broadly into two main categories: the pure supply ship, not fitted with any equipment for anchor-handling or towing, and the much more powerful vessel fully equipped to tow, lay and recover anchors. In addition there are also highly specialised vessels based on supply ship

Soliman Reys *is one of many early oil rig supply vessels, now outmoded in the offshore oil industry, that has found alternative employment in coastal towing and other related work. Operated by Rederij de Bruinvis, she is a vessel of 488 gross tons, 1900 bhp and 28 tonnes bollard pull, built in 1969.* (Author)

designs, but equipped to provide other services in the oil industry. It is the fully equipped anchor-handling supply ship with which we are mainly concerned. The size and power of oil rig supply vessels is determined very much by the location in which they are intended to operate. When this breed of vessel gained prominence in the very early 1960s most had evolved from relatively small ships, by today's standards, in use in the oilfields of the Gulf of Mexico. As offshore oil exploration spread to the Arabian Gulf, the Far East and North Sea, conditions became more demanding with a corresponding need for larger and more powerful supporting vessels. As earlier supply vessels have become outmoded they have found alternative employment as inshore salvage vessels or tugs, where the inherent additional deck space is particularly advantageous.

The modern anchor-handling oil rig supply ship embodies most of the towing and anchor-handling equipment attributed to the anchor-handling tug in earlier paragraphs. Size and cargo capacity are the main and all-important factors. A typical example of an anchor-handling supply vessel working in the northern regions of the North Sea would be a ship of some 2,300 gross tonnes, 74 metres in length, with a long, clear afterdeck capable of carrying 1,200 tonnes of cargo. The cargo carried varies considerably but will include foodstuffs and other stores in standard containers, engineering equipment and often drill pipe, casing and other long cylindrical items in large quantities. In addition, dedicated cargo tanks and handling equipment will be available for cargoes of bulk liquids. The liquid cargoes commonly carried by supply vessels are potable (drinking) water, drilling water, liquid mud, brine and fuel oil. Drilling water, mud and brine are special compounds used in the process of drilling for oil and may need special treatment while on board, such as regular agitation.

The propulsion system of an anchor-handling supply vessel of the type described will certainly be twin screw, with controllable-pitch propellers rotating within fixed Kort nozzles. Four main engines are common, with two driving each propeller shaft through twin input/single output gearboxes. The total power available from this arrangement will average some 16,000 bhp and give the vessel a bollard pull of some 160 tonnes. Transverse thrusters are likely to be fitted fore and aft and possibly an additional, retractable azimuthing thruster in the bow. The propulsion and steering control systems in most modern supply vessels include a single lever "joystick" control, working in conjunction with the main engines, propeller controls and thrusters. As previously mentioned, systems of this kind are computer controlled and also make use of inputs from the vessel's auto-pilot and gyro compass. This enables the ship to be moved bodily in any direction by the movement of a single lever, and the heading to be changed by simply setting a compass bearing. Many of the controls and a "joystick" are provided at an after control station in the wheelhouse with an exceptional view of the afterdeck. The master of an anchor-handling rig supply vessel spends a great deal of his time operating from this position.

When the vessel is employed in the "supply ship" mode of operation, it is literally regarded as a very large and versatile maritime truck. Supplies of all kinds are taken on board in a convenient port and taken to the rig being supported, a journey that might vary in distance between a few dozen or a few hundred miles. At either end of the delivery voyage the vessel will be required

An important feature of the oil rig supply vessel is its ability to manoeuvre easily and safely into position for loading and unloading alongside a rig at sea. In this picture the Smit-Lloyd 109 *(1292 gross tons) is seen attending the semi-submersible rig Ocean Liberator.* (Smit)

to manoeuvre accurately and quickly. In port it may be necessary to move between various berths in order to load different bulk and containerised cargoes. When the vessel arrives at the rig it will be required to take up an allotted position beneath the appropriate crane and unloading area. In most cases this involves moving into position stern-first and remaining in position while unloading takes place. Frequently, no actual mooring is possible and the supply ship must be capable of accurately maintaining the correct position and heading for long periods, sometimes in very difficult weather conditions. In this respect the single-lever control simplifies matters considerably for the ship's master. The vessel is manoeuvred forward, astern and to either side quite easily while the auto-pilot maintains a pre-set heading. If necessary, cargo is moved around the deck by means of wires from the tugger winches. Bulk cargo is transferred by means of hoses, using the powerful pumping equipment installed in the vessel.

When towing, the oil rig supply vessel operates in exactly the same manner as any very large open-stern tug. The afterdeck is of course cleared to ensure that there are no obstructions to foul or interfere with the towline. In most cases hydraulically operated line-handling equipment and stop pins are used to control the position of the towline and prevent it moving out to either side and endangering the vessel. Alternatively a gog eye will be fitted to the deck aft and the wire from a tugger winch used as a gog rope, with a large running shackle in place over the towline.

Many large and powerful oil rig supply vessels are equipped with high-capacity fire-fighting systems and monitors capable of fighting fires on exploration rigs and production platforms. In order to be suitable for this work monitors must be capable of projecting jets of water high enough to reach the upper levels of massive platforms, often over 100 metres high. Supply vessels equipped in this way may well be engaged in a "stand-by" role that also involves rescue duties should a major incident occur on a rig or platform. Among the additional items of equipment needed for the task are small, fast rescue craft, scrambling nets and other aids to retrieving personnel from the water. Some very large vessels are also equipped with a lightweight "heli-deck" to enable helicopters to land and take off to transfer personnel and stores.

Anchor-handling operations

When the oil rig or barge arrives in the desired location, attendant tugs or supply vessels keep it in position until the anchors are laid and known to be holding satisfactorily. Each anchor is connected to a steel wire rope or chain cable deployed by winches aboard the rig, and the entire operation is controlled by the officer in charge of the rig.

There are two main methods of laying and retrieving these large anchors. An early, well-established method involves the use of a steel wire pennant permanently attached to the head of the anchor. The free end of the pennant passes through a large steel buoy and, when the anchor is laid, the buoy and pennant remain attached with the end of the pennant supported on the surface by the buoy, ready to aid retrieval.

A more modern system, developed for use in much deeper water, does not use a buoy. The pennant is attached to a "chaser" – a shaped steel collar that is free to move along the anchor cable and locate on the shank of the anchor. The pennant is used to carry the anchor out to its position, but is "chased" (towed) back to the rig for retention until required for the retrieval operation at a later date.

To lay an anchor, the tug must first take on board the free end of the pennant. The tug manoeuvres close to the anchor stowage position on the rig and the pennant end is passed down to her afterdeck by crane. The pennant is coupled to the anchor-handling winch wire and hauled in until the anchor is secured, hanging beneath the tug's stern roller. If a buoy is used it is taken on deck or also secured at the stern. The tug then moves away from the rig to a predetermined position as the anchor cable is paid out. Once in position, the anchor is lowered to the seabed and towed along to tension the chain cable. The pennant is then secured to its buoy or, when a "chaser" is used, returned to the rig. The operation is repeated until all eight anchors are in position. If the seabed is such that anchors do not hold the rig properly, two anchors may be connected to each anchor cable. This may entail the tug taking the anchors on board, along with their connecting chain, to transport them to the position where they will be laid.

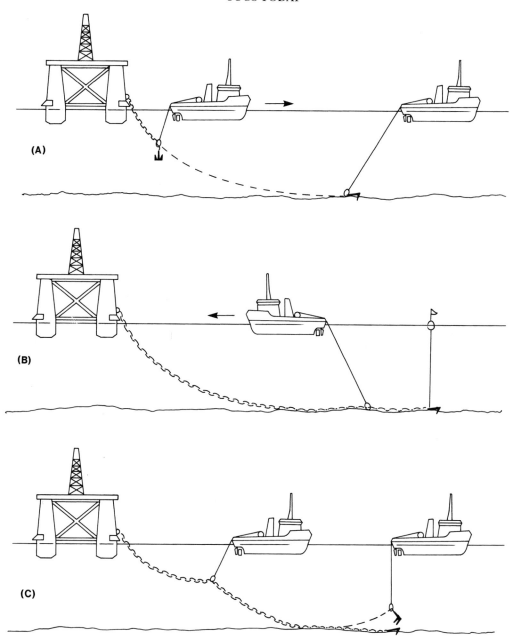

Anchor-handling operations.
a) *The tug, using a "chaser", hauls the pennant and "chaser" under her stern and takes the anchor out to the required position, lowers it to the seabed and tows it out to tension the chain.*
b) *Either, a buoy is secured to a permanently attached pennant, or the "chaser" is towed back to the rig.*
c) *To retrieve the anchor the "chaser" is towed from the rig along the anchor chain to engage the anchor, or the buoyed pennant is retrieved, to haul the anchor from the seabed to be returned to the rig.*

Oil rig supply vessels and anchor-handling tugs must be capable of remaining at sea in all weathers. This spectacular picture shows the bow of anchor-handling supply vessel Star Spica, *of Star Offshore Services Marine Ltd, lifting to a heavy sea.* Star Spica *is a vessel of 1558 gross tons and 9180 bhp, built in 1985.*   *(Ulstein)*

To lift the anchors in readiness for a "rig move", much the same process will be repeated in reverse. A "chaser" pennant is collected from the rig and towed along the anchor cable until it is positioned on the anchor. With a buoy system the pennant is connected to the winch wire and the buoy secured or taken on board. With the pennant connected the tug hauls on the anchor to "break it out" from the seabed. It is then raised and taken back to the rig as the cable is reeled in.

The operation is not always straightforward. If a pennant breaks or for some reason the anchor cannot be retrieved in the normal way, the vessel will have to retrieve the anchor wire by "grappling" for it using a specially designed grappling hook or a device known as a "J" hook. This is a tedious process, involving towing the grapple across the seabed until the wire is "caught" and hauled aboard. The anchor-handler may also be required to service the rig's anchors and replace pennants or anchor cables. Many vessels equipped for anchor-handling are provided with additional, large, power-operated storage drums to enable these items to be taken on board.

Anchor-handling operations must continue day and night in all weathers until the work is completed. It may take a couple of anchor-handling tugs or supply vessels anything from 12 hours to several days to lay a pattern of eight anchors in poor conditions. The crew on the afterdeck may be working for long hours with heavy gear, waist-deep in water with the vessel rolling and pitching in an alarming manner.

CHAPTER 9

Pusher tugs and pushing

A less obvious form of towage, used widely throughout the world, is pushing. Large numbers of vessels spend most of their working lives pushing barges of all shapes and sizes, either on inland waterways or at sea. In some countries the movement of cargo by pusher tug and barge on inland waterways is an important feature of the national transport infrastructure. The tugs employed in this unlikely form of towage fall into two quite distinct breeds. There are the true "pushers", known in American parlance as "towboats", designed to operate almost exclusively on inland waterways; they are invariably rectangular in planform and unlike any other type of tug. There are also tugs of a conventional type that spend much of their working lives pushing. Of these, many operate inland but others form part of sea-going transport system working with very specialised barges or as part of fully integrated tug/barge systems.

Elsewhere in this book the emphasis has been on towing astern, which raises the valid question "Why is pushing so widely used?". There are two main reasons: improved handling and economy, particularly when handling very large loads on inland waters. Once a pusher tug is connected astern of her train of barges the whole tow behaves in much the same way as a single vessel, achieving not only improvements in handling but also in propulsive efficiency and fuel consumption.

The aim of all tug and barge combinations is to maximise the use of the most expensive components of the transport system – the power unit and the crew. One tug can service many barges, delivering cargoes, returning empty craft, or deploying them to other locations to load return cargoes. The tug does not have to remain idle during loading or unloading operations and, if properly organised, can remain in operation more or less continuously. A useful by-product of the barge is that it can provide a convenient means of short-term storage, particularly for bulk cargoes. Once loaded, weather-proofed barges can, if necessary, remain at convenient moorings until required, offering a high degree of security.

For pushing to be effective, the barges must be firmly secured to the bow of the tug and each other; those built for use with pusher tugs have square ends and are easily secured together as a single unit. The manner in which barges are prepared for pushing varies considerably with the waterway and geographical location. In areas where the waterways are mainly narrow rivers or canals, barges are pushed singly or in tows of two or three barges line-ahead. The need to use the largest

The pusher tug Hammonia *is proceeding up the river Rhine from Holland into Germany with four loaded coal barges. Owned by Speksnijder of Papendrecht she is a twin screw tug of 32 metres in length and 2500 bhp, typical of many employed on the European waterways.* (Author)

barges practicable, and handle several with a single tug, has made conventional towing uneconomic on many waterways.

On the major waterways in Europe barges of 5,000 tonnes are regularly pushed for hundreds of miles two abreast in tows of up to six barges. Large American "towboats" handle vast tows of up to 30 barges on the wide rivers of the southern states of the USA. Push-towing on inland waterways is common throughout Europe, America, Africa and some parts of Asia. Many of these areas have wide but sometimes shallow waterways running for many hundreds of miles, acting as major thoroughfares for cargoes moving inland from coastal ports. In Britain the inland waterways are generally very narrow and less suited to push-towing with vessels of any size, resulting in a very small population of true and rather specialised pushers. To undertake push-towing operations under these differing conditions, a wide variety of vessels of different sizes and designs are used, but all operate in a similar manner.

Pushing operations at sea are complicated by weather conditions, which can dramatically affect the performance and safety of the tug and her barge. The tug used in this type of operation is normally of the conventional screw type, suitably modified, or purpose-built for the work. Single barges are used, shaped at the stern to accommodate the bow of the tug. The very sophisticated, fully integrated tug/barge systems closely resemble a ship when assembled, with the tug fitting closely on to the stern of the vessel.

The pusher tug
The true pusher tug comes in a variety of shapes and sizes, but virtually all are based on a hull that is rectangular in shape. Above the waterline the bow is square and incorporates two or more heavily fendered vertical "push knees", forming the tug's interface with her tow. The knees are often several metres high to enable good contact to be made with the barges being pushed, regardless of whether they are

Ordale H is the only large European pusher tug in use in Britain, where she pushes tank barges loaded with Orimulsion on the river Mersey. This view shows her rectangular shape, two stern anchors, workboat and the wires securing her to her barges. Orignally built in Holland as the Willem Barendsz *in 1971, she is a triple screw vessel of 35.05 metres in length with main engines producing 3900 bhp. She is owned by J Harker Ltd.*   *(Author)*

fully loaded and deep in the water or empty with a great deal of freeboard. Steps are constructed in the rear face of the knees or a special ladder provided to enable crew members to gain access to the barge's decks, whatever their height.

The methods used to secure the barges to each other and to the tug vary greatly with the geographical location and with the individual operator. Steel wire ropes are generally used to make the various towing connections, but an important feature of the operation is the means used to tension the securing wires. Throughout Europe and in many other locations small deck winches are fitted at strategic locations on the pusher tugs and aboard the barges; these are generally hand-operated via large distinctive handwheels and are designed to produce the required tension in wires connecting the barges to each other and to the tug with little manual effort. Similar winches are frequently installed on multi-purpose work vessels and small conventional screw tugs to facilitate pushing operations. Tensioning devices using a screw thread, known as "steamboat ratchets", are still widely used in pushing operations in the USA among the "towboat community" for the same purpose.

The height of the barges being pushed and the length of the tow stretching out ahead of the tug presents a problem of visibility for all tug masters involved in pushing operations. A good field of view forward over the barges is essential, bearing in mind that the bow of the first barge may be many metres away from the tug. This demands a wheelhouse mounted at a suitable height; in some areas the provision of these presents no difficulty, while in others it conflicts with the need to pass under low bridges or through tunnels. Various forms of retractable wheelhouse are used to combat this problem; most are hydraulically operated and can be readily varied in height to suit operating conditions while the vessel is under way.

The propulsion system is invariably of the conventional screw type, with the number of propellers dependent on the size of the vessel and power output required. A twin-screw arrangement is most common, but triple and quadruple installations are by no means rare. Multiple rudders astern and additional "flanking" rudders located ahead of the propellers are frequently used to enhance the vessel's handling characteristics. Fixed Kort nozzles are often used to improve performance, and in very shallow draught tugs the propellers may be recessed in tunnels beneath the hull. In some of the smaller tugs azimuthing propulsion units are used instead of normal propellers to enhance their manoeuvrability. The power output of the engines will depend on the size of tug, but can vary from 120 bhp in the smallest canal pusher to more than 6,000 bhp in a very large "towboat". Unlike most other tugs, inland waterways craft often have completely self-contained engine cooling systems to avoid the possibility of picking up debris and foreign matter, a common source of trouble in shallow waters. A great curse of the conventional cooling system is the discarded plastic bag, which can cause havoc once sucked into the tug's hull inlet. Instead of drawing cooling water from outside the vessel the skin of the vessel or tubes under the hull are used to dissipate heat from the engine systems.

The wheelhouse on the pusher tug Danelle, *operated by Hadumar, is just one of many innovative designs found in European vessels. In the picture the wheelhouse is extended to it's full height to enable the tug's master to see forward over the container barges being pushed upriver from Rotterdam. (Author)*

There are occasions when the pusher tug will need to anchor. Most have one or two anchors, located at the stern and controlled by a windlass in the normal way. These anchors are generally larger than those normally found on inland vessels to ensure that they are capable of holding not only the tug but also a heavy tow, should an emergency arise. A towing hook may also be fitted at the after end of some pusher tugs, used to handle individual craft when the tug is preparing barges for a journey.

Small pushers

The smallest pusher tugs of all are relatively simple vessels, consisting of little more than a hull, engines and wheelhouse, with often no requirement for more than rudimentary accommodation. Measuring between 5 and 15 metres in length, with engines of 200–500 bhp, they have many uses. In most parts of the world, where large-scale push-towing is carried out, small pusher tugs are employed to assemble strings of barges in readiness for the larger tugs. This entails collecting barges one or two at a time from loading and discharging wharves and travelling short distances to and from the assembly point.

In the United Kingdom cargoes of stone, coal, fertilisers, paper products and animal feedstuff are transported by barge on the very narrow inland waterways. Motive power is provided by small pusher tugs or small conventional tugs equipped for pushing. Operating with barges of only 80–100 tons, they require engines of no more than 120–250 bhp. The size of barge and their attendant tugs is limited by the dimensions of the canals and their lock systems, which were originally designed for self-propelled traditional "narrow boats".

SCH2220 is a very small pusher tug, from the large fleet of Deutsch Binnenreederei of Berlin, used to handle individual barges on the inland waterways in Germany. Only 10 metres in length she is powered by a single engine of 140 bhp driving a steerable out drive unit. Note the single tensioning winch between her push knees. The tug is in operation in Britain in a joint venture between her owners and A C Bennet & Sons Ltd of Rochester. (Author)

The tug Hippolyte Bloch *is one of a fleet of powerful vessels, operated by the French company C.G.N.R. pushing barges from the major ports in Holland through Germany and into France.* H Bloch *is a triple screw vessel of 32 metres in length and 4800 bhp.*   *(Lawrence Amboldt)*

European pushers

Several hundred pusher tugs are employed throughout Europe on the inland waterways systems. Of these many are medium-sized pusher tugs or conventional tugs fitted with push knees, serving the shorter routes and feeder services. Large well-equipped pusher tugs undertake the longer-distance tows with up to six large barges of perhaps 2,000–5,000 tons each. A vessel of similar size, in use on the major rivers of America, would be regarded as a medium-sized craft and employed on the shorter routes.

The configuration chosen by European owners is determined very much by the regular routes on which the vessel will be used. The size of the waterway, its locks and bridge heights and the regulations applying to the particular waterway are all factors to be considered. Power requirements are governed by the size of the barges and likely tidal conditions. The result is likely to be a vessel of between 15 and 40 metres in length and up to 5,000 bhp. Twin or triple screws are the most common arrangement, with Kort nozzles and multiple rudder systems. Flanking rudders are used in conjunction with the normal steering and propeller controls to achieve a high degree of manoeuvrability.

As previously mentioned, wheelhouse height can be critical, and even on the larger vessels some form of variable-height structure may be fitted. This may take the form of a straightforward vertical lifting wheelhouse or one incorporating a more complex mechanism. Most are hydraulically operated and in the lowered position blend with the superstructure. The vessel's radar antenna and masts are also capable of being raised and lowered. Two high-definition radars are often installed in the larger tugs, enabling operations to continue in poor weather.

A feature of this larger type of vessel is the high standard of accommodation provided. Many of the European inland waterways tugs, and indeed many self-propelled craft, are operated and manned by family concerns and become a mobile home to those on board. As a result there are often signs of domestic accoutrements and family life aboard. Small boats may be carried to act as tenders and workboats in the normal manner, but in addition it is not unusual to see a car parked on the afterdeck, with a small crane or ramps provided for loading and unloading.

American-style "towboats"

The origin of the large American towboat can be traced back to the days of the early stern-wheel paddle-craft that plied the wide shallow waterways of the southern states. Their modern counterparts are an important part of the transport network, moving many thousands of tons of cargo on rivers flowing through the heart of the country. Many old-established companies operate sophisticated modern towboats on the Mississippi, Missouri, Ohio and Tennessee rivers and their tributaries.

The configuration of these giants is basically the same as their smaller European sisters, but again the difference is in the scale of the entire operation. The towboats vary in size from the smaller types of vessel previously mentioned to very large craft of over 50 metres in length and 14 metres beam; such vessels may have a draught of less than 3 metres. The power required to handle the very large tows undertaken by many tugs often exceeds 6,500 bhp, and twin-, triple- and quadruple-screw propulsion arrangements are common. The most striking feature of the large towboat is the hotel-like accommodation, housed in a huge

This impressive tow of sixteen coal barges is typical of many such tows moving bulk cargoes on the rivers of the USA. Mixed tows of full and empty barges of twice this number are not unusual. The towboat is a triple screw vessel from the fleet of the Mid South Towing Company. (Ship & Boat Int)

The towboat Mississippi *was built for the US Corps of Engineers by Halter Marine in 1993. She is a triple screw vessel of 88.70 metres in length powered by three Caterpillar main engines producing 7000 bhp.* *(Ship & Boat Int)*

superstructure three or four decks high. The wheelhouse surmounts this massive structure, providing the master with an uninterrupted all-round view. A number of powerful searchlights are provided to illuminate the margins of the waterway when necessary and to inspect the tow.

The routes travelled can be many hundreds of miles long and the tow being pushed may contain over 30,000 tons of cargo and can comprise 20, 30 or even 50 barges containing a variety of cargoes. Some, however, will be empty, and this presents its own problems. In order to make up a balanced, manageable tow, the barges will be assembled with the heavier units in the centre and lighter ones around the sides. Also to be considered is the destination of each barge; some will be detached at intermediate ports and others picked up en route.

The use of large pushing towboats is not confined to the USA, and many other parts of the world have waterways equally suited to this form of transport. For instance, the Nile and several other rivers in Africa and Asia have similar systems in operation.

Double-ended tugs

A small but notable minority of tugs, employed mainly in Europe, are designed as true "double-ended" vessels, being fully equipped for pushing and towing. The more modern double-ended tugs are vessels of 500–1,000 bhp and about 25 metres in length, and a hull design with push knees at one end and a conventional bow at the other makes them unique. Tractor propulsion is used, generally with azimuthing propulsion units located beneath the bow. Such vessels are incredibly agile and have a wide range of uses.

When pushing, the vessel places her knees against the tow and is secured in the normal way. For towing astern a tow hook or winch is fitted forward of the knees; the towline emerges through an aperture between the knees and the vessel travels bow-first. In most true double-ended vessels the controls in the wheelhouse and

The small pusher tug Saar Louis *is seen pushing four Lighter Aboard Ship barges through the Rhine gorge, many miles from the "mother ship's" terminal in Holland. The barges are secured to each other using their own tensioning winches and a small false bow has been added to improve their towing characteristics.* (Author)

the vessel's towing and navigation lights are all designed to allow her to travel safely in both directions.

Working with ship-borne barges

There are a number of transport systems that employ barges of a uniform design that are transported between major shipping centres around the world aboard very large purpose-built ships. The barges vary in size between approximately 400 and 800 tonnes and are completely rectangular in shape. A very familiar example, known as the "Lighter Aboard Ship" (LASH) system, is used to transport paper products between North America and Europe. Once the ship arrives at the terminal port small pusher tugs are used to marshal the barges and distribute them for unloading and loading, often to wharves some distance away; many do not handle particularly well due to their box-like shape. The barges are equipped with small tensioning winches at each corner and are made up into a single tow in the usual way. If the barges are to be pushed for any great distance a small "false bow" made be added to the front of the first barge to improve the handling characteristics of the tow.

Pushing with conventional tugs

Conventional screw tugs are used in large numbers for push-towing on inland waterways and at sea. This form of operation offers great flexibility, often allowing the most suitable mode of operation, pushing or towing, to be chosen with little additional preparation.

Small conventional tugs and tug/workboats are very popular for pushing operations in Europe and elsewhere in the world. This means of providing motive power for single or small numbers of barges and construction plant is particularly economical when relatively short journeys are involved. The tugs used are often adapted for the work, or purpose-built.

Many of those employed on inland waterways are comparatively elderly and have very long working lives; operating in fresh water reduces the effects of corrosion on hulls, slowing down the rate of deterioration significantly, and it is not unusual for a vessel to be updated and a new engine fitted at intervals of perhaps 20 years. The tugs themselves are little different from those described in previous chapters. To adapt them for push-towing a single strengthened knee is fitted to the bow. An alternative arrangement comprises a simple frame with fendering fitted, closely resembling the knees of a true pusher tug. Again, small hand winches are fitted to tension the wires securing the tug to her barge. Pushing on a single knee demands great care in securing and tensioning the wires, which run diagonally from the after corners of the barge to the winches on the tug's afterdeck. In general the barges used are of the flat-stern type or more elderly rounded barges adapted for pushing. As with the pushers previously mentioned, the height of the wheelhouse is of prime importance, and additional flying bridges or ingenious variable-height wheelhouses are fitted in much the same way.

This method of towing is common in the USA on the smaller rivers and canals and in coastal waters. Many of the barges used have a shallow notch provided in the stern in which the bow of the tug is inserted, in much the same manner as larger sea-going craft. In smaller American tugs the securing wires are tensioned using the traditional "steamboat ratchets" or by using the towing winch.

Many small tugs in Europe, such as the tug/workboat Andre, *spend much of their time pushing. It has proved to be an efficient means of employing relatively low powered vessels to handle barges and construction plant.* Andre *is a single screw vessel of 365 bhp, owned by F W Bouwman &* *Sons of Zerikzee in Holland.* (Author)

Elfer Guidry is a coastal tug fully equipped to push or tow. In the picture she is pushing a tank barge without a notch. Note the high level wheelhouse, towing winch and after control position. The tug is a triple screw vessel of 199 gross tons built in 1968 and currently owned by Lockport Tugs Inc. Houma. (Michael Vincent)

Push-towing at sea

Pushing rather than towing barges at sea is popular on many coastal and intercontinental routes. This method of operation, with a conventional screw tug pushing a barge, was originally developed in North America where barges were regularly pushed on inshore waters for a great many years. More recently purpose-built barges, with a deep notch located at the stern to accept the tug's bow, have become a well-established method of operation in many parts of the world.

Tug and barge transport systems of this type have been adopted by companies in Scandinavia, Northern Europe and in the Middle and Far East on coastal and deep-sea routes. The method is particularly suited to bulk cargoes, with coal, ore, stone, crude oil and petroleum products being the most common. Specially constructed carriers are used to carry timber, forest products, cars, containers and cattle. Such barges of 10,000 to 20,000 tons with many advanced features are becoming common. Once the tug is secured in position at the after end of the barge it operates in much the same way as a small ship. Remote controls are provided to enable the tug master to lower and raise the barge's anchors, control the various lights, stop and start auxiliary engines, and in some cases operate a bow thrust unit. These remote controls may be operated via an "umbilical" cable when the tug is pushing the barge or by a radio link when it is streamed astern on a towline.

The tugs engaged in this type of work are what may be described as medium-sized conventional screw vessels. Most have a twin-screw propulsion system with fixed or steerable Kort nozzles and often controllable-pitch propellers. The power required varies with the size of barge and the conditions in which it will operate, but vessels of between 2,500 and 6,000 bhp are typical. In most respects they are equipped in exactly the same manner as a large ship-handling or coastal tug. As previously mentioned, many American tugs regularly perform both ship-handling and barge-towing duties. The question of visibility forward over the barge is again an important one. Tugs regularly engaged in push-towing large barges can readily be identified by a high-level control position of some kind. A popular arrangement takes the form of a secondary wheelhouse mounted high above the normal one. Access to this "crow's nest"-type wheelhouse is via an external ladder or stairs inside the vertical column. Variable-height wheelhouses, similar in design to those of inland vessels, are also used by some owners.

Suitable bow fendering is essential and often the shape of the bow is designed to match the notches of a particular series of barges. Unlike vessels involved in fully integrated tug/barge systems, the tugs employed are frequently required to operate with a wide range of barges. The method used to couple the tug and barge together is a critical factor in sea-going tug and barge operation, and much effort has gone into developing suitable methods and equipment. The ideal form of coupling is one that allows the tug to be quickly and positively attached to the stern of the barge, and compensates automatically for changes in draught of the tug or barge. The most usual compromise is to have a moderately deep notch in the stern of the barge and a wire rope securing system utilising the tug's towing winch to provide the necessary tension. A common method of retaining the tug firmly in the notch of the barge uses two wires, one from each after quarter of the

This impressive picture of the Morton S Bouchard *of New York shows the tug secured in the deep notch of a tank barge by wires from her after quarters. The barge is in a very light condition, demonstrating the need for a high level wheelhouse.* Morton S Bouchard *is a tug of 3900 bhp built in 1975.* (Michael Vincent)

barge; the ends of the wires are secured aboard the barge and passed through heavy fairleads in the bulwarks of the tug near the stern. The inner ends are then shackled to a towline from the towing winch and tension applied, drawing the tug forward to engage the barge's notch firmly.

There are a number of proven alternative methods of coupling the tug and barge together to form a single unit. One popular system makes use of hydraulically operated pins or other latching devices, fitted on either side of the tug's bow, to engage in vertical grooves in the sides of the barge's notch. Variations of this basic system include the ability to engage positively the locking devices in teeth in the vertical grooves, or control the relative vertical movement between the two vessels by means of hydraulically controlled friction pads. In either case the tug is positively located on the centreline of the barge but allowed some pitching movement. Such systems have the advantage of being quick to operate and, depending on the type used, may offer some vertical freedom of movement between the tug and barge. Although many tugs are fitted with coupling systems similar to those described, they may only be used with barges of the same type or with precisely matching couplings.

A further variation of the above system is one that incorporates a third locking pin or device in the bow of the tug. When engaged, this effectively controls any pitching movement, making the connection completely rigid. This arrangement is most often applied to the fully integrated tug/barge systems described later.

The tug remains connected to the stern of the barge for the duration of its intended voyage, unless the weather conditions deteriorate beyond certain predetermined criteria. It is generally the state of the sea that limits the safety of the tug/barge combination in the pushing mode. The criteria laid down vary with the particular craft and type of coupling involved, but a wave height of

The Danish company Em Z Svitzer of Copenhagen operate a number of bulk cargo services around northern Europe using barges such as the Odin *(1400 dwt) shown here in ballast. In this case motive power is provided by the single screw tug* Valkyrien, *a vessel of 291 gross tons and 3700 bhp. The tug and barge are coupled together using an hydraulically operated "Articouple" system.* (Author)

Groton *is an integrated tug/barge unit, one of a number operated by the Amerada Hess Corporation between the Virgin Islands and the US mainland. Built in 1982, the tug is a twin hulled vessel of 40.75 metres in length linked with a "ship shaped" oil tank barge of 22471 gross tons.* (Michael Vincent)

approximately 2–3 metres is likely to be the limit imposed on many tug/barge combinations using wire rope systems. Once this sea state is reached the tug will disengage from the notch in the barge to prevent damage to the connecting wires or to the vessels themselves. A normal towline will have been rigged on the barge in readiness for such an eventuality and arranged to enable the tug to take up a towing position ahead of the barge with a minimum of effort or lost time.

Integrated tug and barge units

The fully integrated tug and barge unit takes the tug and barge principle described in the preceding paragraphs one stage further. The combination of tug and matching barges is designed to operate exclusively as a transport system in its own right. The tug is no longer a readily adaptable workhorse, but a dedicated power unit for a certain number of barges. Once assembled the tug and barge are to all intents and purposes a ship. In operation, two tugs may typically service four or five specially constructed barges. At the end of each voyage the tug simply leaves one barge and collects another for the return journey. Thus the expensive "power unit" and her crew are fully utilised.

The means of coupling such vessels to their respective barges remains controversial in some sections of the towage industry. There are broadly two approaches to achieving the necessary interface. The most common is a development of the tug and barge systems previously described, where the tug is engaged in a very deep notch in the barge; it is not unusual for the tug to enter the notch for more than half its own length. An alternative design utilises a tug based on a catamaran configuration, the forward end of which locates on the outside of the specially shaped stern of its barge. Whichever design is used, the connection between the two units will be fully rigid and accomplished by some form of hydraulic locking mechanism. Once the tug is in position, electrical and hydraulic power supplies are connected to enable the various pieces of ancillary equipment on the barge to be operated directly from the tug's systems. With the most modern fully integrated tug and barge systems there is no provision for the tug to be disengaged at sea or for her to tow the barge astern.

Index